The Guide to Successful
Tapestry Weaving

The Guide to Successful

Tapestry Weaving

by Nancy Harvey

Pacific Search Press

Pacific Search Press, 222 Dexter Avenue North
    Seattle, Washington 98109
© 1981 by Nancy Harvey. All rights reserved.
Printed in the United States of America

Edited by Betsy Rupp Fulwiler
Designed by Judy Petry

Cover photo: *Detail of tapestry woven by the author*

Library of Congress Cataloging in Publication Data

Harvey, Nancy.
    The guide to successful tapestry weaving.

    Bibliography: p.
    Includes index.
    1. Hand weaving.   2. Tapestry.   I. Title.
TT848.H377   746.3   81-2103
ISBN 0-914718-55-X   AACR2

To my husband, Donald,
for his constant support and encouragement;
to my two best friends, Eric and Kristine;
and in memory of my sister-in-law Virginia Cureton.

CONTENTS

I would like to express my sincere thanks and heartfelt appreciation to the many people who helped me with this book:

The friends and students who reviewed the text, wove the sample project in this book, and offered their valuable comments.

The artists, designers, and tapestry weavers who so graciously shared photographs of their tapestries to inspire us all.

Jean Hessler, who provided me with so much beautiful handspun yarn.

Randy De Luchi, who took time from his busy senior year of high school to prepare the two pen and ink sketches.

Alix Peshette, who contributed so much interest and information to the chapter about tapestry design.

My good friend Mary Running, who actually came running whenever I needed two more hands for whatever purpose.

The staff at the San Francisco Tapestry Workshop who shared techniques and traditions as well as their own personal discoveries.

My friends at Yarn and Weavers Things in Sacramento who answered countless questions and allowed me to photograph looms, equipment, and materials.

Special thanks to Hal Painter and Jim Brown, who introduced me to tapestry weaving, shared their ideas and knowledge with me, cared about my efforts, and motivated and inspired me in my work.

WHAT THIS GUIDE IS ALL ABOUT

WHAT IS TAPESTRY WEAVING?

Tapestry weaving has had a long life and, fortunately for us, it has managed to survive the ravages of time. Remnants of fabric have been found in Egypt, indicating that tapestries were woven as early as 3000 B.C. Regardless of where these early tapestries were woven, or what type of loom (horizontal or vertical) was used, the techniques were very similar and have remained basically unchanged throughout history.

In most countries, ancient tapestries were designed by famous artists, who painted full-scale, colored cartoons or design patterns, which professional weavers transformed into beautiful tapestries. Generally, these early period tapestries had a somewhat coarse texture. They were woven mainly of wool, although silk and even gold threads sometimes were incorporated. Through the ages, tapestries became very painterly in appearance—using thousands of colors in a single piece—and were so fine in texture that they hardly appeared to be woven.

Contemporary tapestries are no longer always a copy of a finished picture. Designs have been simplified, using fewer colors and again a coarser weave. There is also more freedom and flexibility today. Many weavers

1. *The Navajo Indians, famous for their woven rugs, weave on a primitive vertical loom. (Illustration by Randy De Luchi)*

1.

tapestry is also the weaver.

Although tapestry weaving is thought to have been done only quite recently in North America, there is evidence that some American Indian tribes have been weaving for more than a thousand years. The Navajo Indians, for example, have been utilizing true tapestry techniques for the past several hundred years in the weaving of their beautiful blankets and rugs, making a valuable contribution to the art. It is believed that they learned from the Pueblos, whose weaving began a thousand years before. The tapestry weaving techniques used in making Navajo rugs are similar to those used in other countries. However, a cartoon is not used and the intricate design emerges, almost magically, from within the head of the weaver. A special warping process produces a bound edge all the way around the rug. Because weft ends are completely woven in as they are added (many other techniques leave the ends extending on the wrong side of the piece), the rug is also reversible (fig. 3). The rugs are always woven on a vertical loom. The weft is handspun wool, usually dyed with natural dyes from native plants.

Today you find tapestry weavers using both horizontal and vertical looms. In all cases, the weaving is done completely by hand. The warp (the threads wound on the loom in preparation for weaving) is completely covered by the weft (the threads that cross over and under the warp). The weft is wound into butterflies (small skeins) or onto tapestry bobbins or shuttles in preparation for weaving. The rows of weft are packed in place with a hand-held tool or with the beater on the loom.

Traditional tapestries were usually woven sideways, with the wrong side of the tapestry facing the weaver. This meant that the cartoon for the particular

2. *Navajo rug in "Two Gray Hills" pattern. These rugs are woven on a handspun wool warp, with handspun wool weft. Only the black, which is dyed, is not a natural fleece color. (Woven by Ellen Len. From the collection of the author)*

2.

combine a variety of yarns and techniques that have been passed on by many cultures. In many cases, as is especially true in the United States, the designer of the

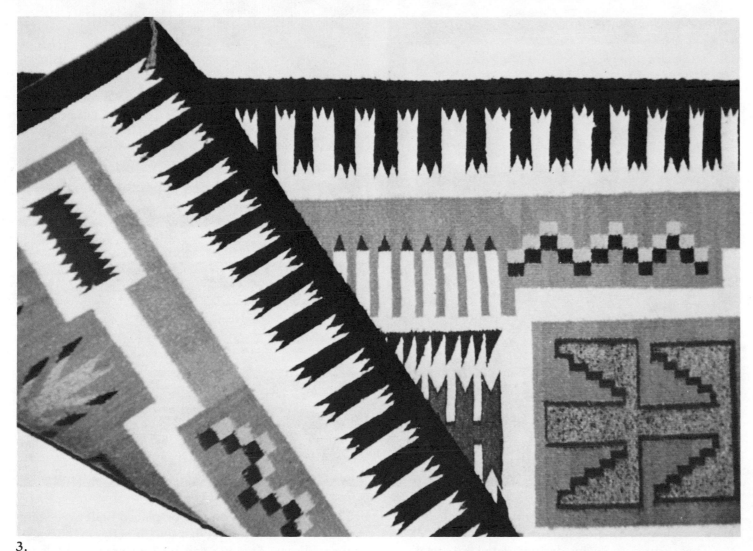

3.

3. *The Navajo rug is bound on all four edges and the weft ends are woven in during weaving, making the rug completely reversible. This rug is woven in the "Storm Pattern" design. (Weaver unknown. From the collection of the author)*

woven piece had to be drawn in reverse, as a mirror image of the completed tapestry (fig. 4). Contemporary weavers frequently weave from the bottom to the top, with the right side facing them as they weave. The actual weaving sequence can be accomplished by weaving a complete row at a time across the entire width of the

5.

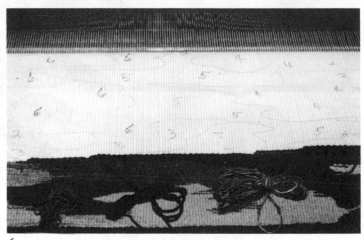

6.

4.

4. *When using a full-scale cartoon and weaving from the back side of the tapestry, the cartoon (above) is the reverse image of the completed tapestry (below).*

5. *A tapestry can be woven one row at a time across the width of the tapestry.*

6. *Building up a design area at a time is another way to weave a tapestry.*

tapestry, using a number of discontinuous wefts (fig. 5), or by building up one design area at a time (fig. 6).

The cartoon may be drawn, detail by detail, in color or in a simple black-and-white outline. Design areas, whether painted or not, are numbered to correspond to the color of weft that will be used in that par-

ticular area. The cartoon can be placed under the warp threads or the design can be drawn directly on the warp, or a small-scale drawing can be kept next to the loom and used only as a reference.

With all these variations, the term "tapestry" has a broader meaning than it once did. While contemporary weavers still weave traditional flat-surfaced tapestries, many weavers are incorporating a variety of other interesting and unusual techniques and textures in their tapestries. In general, "tapestry" now means a weft-faced weave that has been woven completely by hand (rather than being loom controlled) and cannot be reproduced by machines. It can be either one sided (having a definite right and wrong side, with weft ends on the back side) or two sided (where both sides are the same, with weft ends woven in). Many individual design areas make up the total composition. Since tapestries are most often made to hang on a wall, they are sometimes called "handwoven wallhangings." However, do not let this confuse you, because all handwoven wallhangings are not tapestries.

As we continue to rediscover tapestry weaving, we are finding that tapestries not only serve their original purpose—adding warmth to a room and providing a beautiful covering for a bare wall—but they also add a special feeling of comfort and restfulness to our surroundings and illuminate our lives with a remarkable beauty, a kind of "textured poetry."

THE NEED FOR A GUIDE

After several years of weaving and spinning, I was introduced to tapestry weaving and immediately became obsessed with this fascinating art form. As I pursued my obsession, I found it difficult to find answers to all the "what would happen if" questions that were racing around in my head. The only way to learn about tapestry weaving seemed to be to weave—and weave and weave—which is exactly what I did. Finding myself committed, I spent five or six hours a day weaving, experimenting, designing, and studying every aspect of the techniques.

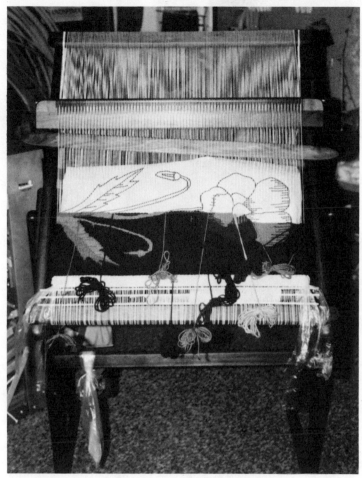

7.

7. *A cartoon, in black-and-white outline, is placed under the warp. This tapestry is being woven sideways, with the right side facing the weaver.*

Having a somewhat analytical mind and experience as an education development analyst for IBM, I decided to analyze and document this search for answers to my many questions. What happens with each row, each design area, and the warp and weft? Why does it happen? What results do I get when I do it differently? Why

8.

8. *Warping a traditional low warp Aubusson tapestry loom is a time-consuming and exacting process. The cartoon is placed under the warp and the tapestry is woven from the back. (Loom designed and built by Jean-Pierre Larochette at the Open Hand Workshop in Berkeley, California. Photo courtesy of the San Francisco Tapestry Workshop)*

do certain things happen one time and not the next? What is good quality? What is the most efficient way to weave a flat-surfaced tapestry without sacrificing technical quality?

Each piece I wove became a valuable and sometimes painful learning experience and included many hours of trial and error learning. I kept thinking, "If only I had known this before." As my study continued, I found that many other weavers—both those who were beginning their investigation of tapestry and those who were already well into the techniques—were experiencing these same feelings. I wanted to share with them the technical and timesaving tips that I had learned. I also

realized that everyone who weaves a tapestry can contribute to the development of the art through their own interpretation and creativity. Why, then, should they have to spend so much time reinventing the basic techniques that they have little or no time and energy left for creativity?

My interest in the educational possibilities grew rapidly. Just what does a beginner need to know to get started? What tips will eliminate all that trial and error learning of the basics? Are there additional techniques that will challenge the experienced tapestry weaver to explore further? What is inspiration and how can it be applied to tapestry design?

The Guide to Successful Tapestry Weaving is the result of all my questioning and experimenting. It is designed to teach you both the basic techniques and solutions to technical problems that you might encounter when beginning, as well as advanced techniques that offer additional challenges you may want to understand and experiment with after you have woven a few tapestries. There are many different approaches to this art, many "right" ways of doing it. If you like a certain approach—it feels right and you achieve the results you want—then do it. Be inventive. Remember that tapestry is a weaving technique—what *you* do with it is what counts.

HOW THIS GUIDE WORKS

The next three chapters of this book will help you get started on the right track by taking you through the various stages involved in weaving a tapestry from start to finish. (Although I intend here to teach you many techniques that work well, I do not imply that they are the only or the best methods.) Technical quality is emphasized and tips and reviews are presented along the way to help you achieve success. For those who are already experienced in weaving techniques, it is suggested, whenever it is appropriate, that you skip the basic instructions of a particular section and proceed to the next section.

After you have completed the sample tapestry, you will be ready for the more advanced information found in the rest of the book. "A Quick Review—And A Lot More" summarizes the weaving sequence and the tips presented in the three preceding chapters. If you need a

9. *This high warp loom is a vertical version of the Aubusson low warp as it uses heddle bars attached to foot treadles. It is not a traditional high warp or Gobelin loom. (Loom designed and built by Jean-Pierre Larochette at the Open Hand Workshop in Berkeley, California. Photo courtesy of the San Francisco Tapestry Workshop)*

10. *The "Gobelin" is a large vertical tapestry loom made by Nilus Leclerc. The loom has string heddles that are hand operated. It does not have harnesses or foot treadles.*

9.

10.

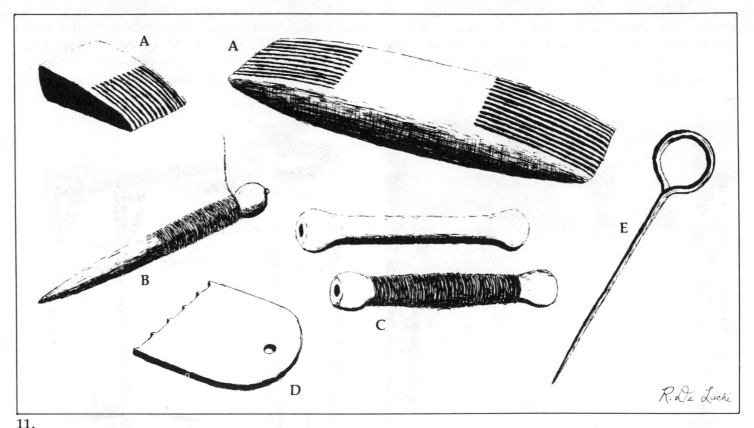

R. De Luchi

11. *Traditional tapestry tools include: packing combs (A); shuttle, which carries weft through the shed, and the tip is used to pack weft in place (B); bobbins for carrying weft (C); scraper for packing weft (D); and an awl for evening out warp spacing (E).*

11.

12. *At the National Wool Showcase in Orland, California, a beginner gets some assistance as she tries her hand at tapestry weaving.*

little help or a few reminders as you start your next tapestries, this chapter will act as a convenient reference, eliminating the necessity of going through the first part of the book. If you have woven tapestries before, you might want to skip all the basic weaving instructions and simply start with this chapter. It also includes many techniques that are not used in the sample project. Each one is described and suggestions are given for how each might be used. Additional methods, besides those presented for the sample tapestry, for

finishing and mounting tapestries are explained in "Finishing, Mounting, and Tapestry Care."

Then we go on to the chapters about creativity. "Inspiration" presents a small sampling of the wide variety of tapestries being woven today in the United States, both by professional tapestry weavers and by those who do it simply for fun. The designers and/or weavers comment about techniques and materials used in their tapestries, indicating the infinite possibilities available in designing and weaving tapestries. Then

"Creating a Design" gives you some ideas and guidelines for getting started on creating your own unique tapestries.

For your convenience, I have also included a chapter about places from which you can order looms and other weaving supplies. A final chapter, "Further Reading," offers a selection of books and magazines that you might find useful.

The tapestries shown in this book were woven by me except those that have the name of another weaver and/or designer credited in the caption.

I hope that by sharing thoughts, offering guidelines that help prevent problems, and explaining not only the "how tos" but also the "whys" in a logical sequence that this book will answer your many questions. I hope, also, that it will help you learn, more quickly and successfully, how to use the techniques, control different yarns, and identify potential problems before they occur, therefore leaving you plenty of time for creativity.

Regardless of how many tapestries you weave, remember that each one of them will be a learning experience and that you probably will be your worst critic. It takes a while to get everything exactly the way you want it. If you do not achieve the desired results the first or second time, it does not mean you are not good—it just means you need a little practice. I once heard someone say that a musician's practice disappears but a weaver's practice just piles up. He was right. But even though our practice does not disappear (and I have a closet full of "practice" to prove it), it all can be worthwhile if we learn from it. To be successful we must take a chance, make a commitment, and then take time to improve.

Now, let's get started!

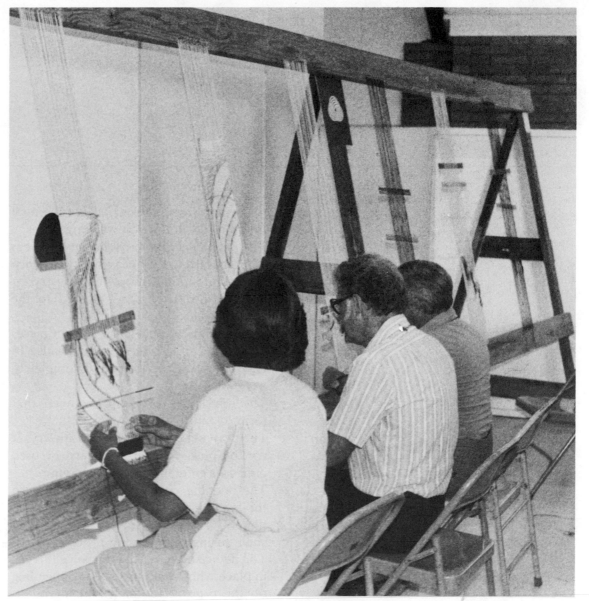

12.

2

THE BASICS

FIRST THINGS FIRST

To make the learning process easier, take time now to learn the meaning of the following weaving terms.

Warp The yarn or threads wound on the loom in preparation for weaving. The warp forms the foundation of the tapestry.

Tension Uniform stretch that is applied to the warp threads.

Weft The fiber going across the woven piece, over and under the warp threads. In tapestry weaving, the weft completely covers the warp.

Weaving The interlacing of warp and weft that forms a fabric.

Cartoon The drawing or design of the tapestry. It can be placed under the warp or used only as a reference during weaving.

Shed The opening created between the warp threads by raising every other warp thread. The weft travels through the shed during the weaving process.

Heddle The device used to hold the warp threads in place when making a shed. Depending on the type of loom, the heddle is at-tached to either a harness, a heddle bar, or a dowel, or the heddle can be a complete device that is commonly referred to as a rigid heddle.

Harness The frame that contains the heddles, except in the case of a rigid heddle.

Treadles The foot-controlled levers used to raise and lower harnesses to make a shed. Looms with rigid heddles do not use foot treadles as the rigid heddle bars are hand operated.

Batten or sword A flat stick that holds the shed open. It is commonly used on primitive vertical looms, some portable frame looms, and looms with rigid heddle bars.

Shuttle A device used to carry the weft through the shed. Some shuttles contain bobbins and the entire shuttle is used to carry the weft. However, this type of shuttle is generally not used in tapestry weaving.

Bobbin A spool around which the weft is wound. Traditional tapestry weavers use wooden bobbins instead of shuttles or butterflies to pass the weft through the shed.

Butterfly	A small skein of weft made by winding the yarn around the fingers. The yarn pulls out from the center of the butterfly as it is passed through the shed, eliminating the necessity for bobbins or shuttles.
Bubbling	Loosely laying the weft in the shed.
Fork or comb	Hand-held tool used to pack the weft in place.
Pack	Pressing the rows of weft close together with a hand-held tool or the beater part of the loom.
Beater	The frame part of the loom that holds the reed. It is used to beat (or pack) the weft in place when a hand-held tool is not used.
Reed	The part of the beater through which the warp is threaded. It is used to space the warp threads. The number of the reed indicates the number of spaces or dents per inch. For example, a twelve-dent reed has twelve spaces per inch.
Dent	The number of spaces per inch in the reed. If you are using a loom with a reed, the number of dents per inch must be the same as the number of warp ends required per inch in your tapestry.
Ends per inch	The number of warp threads per inch, commonly abbreviated as "epi."
Row or pick	The passage of one line of weft through the shed.
Pass	The passage of two lines of weft through the shed.
Plain weave	The weft passes over one warp and under the next.
Heading	The beginning band that is woven prior to starting the tapestry in order to space the warp threads evenly.

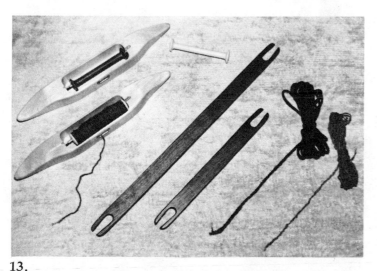

13.

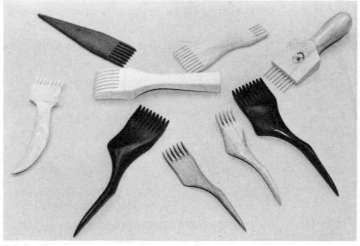

14.

13. *These tools are used to pass the weft through the shed. From left to right (in pairs):* boat shuttles with bobbins; stick shuttles; and butterflies.

14. *Forks or combs for packing the weft in place come in all shapes and sizes.*

15.

15. A reed holds the warp in place and is used on a loom that has a beater. The warp is threaded through the dents (spaces) in the reed.

16. The "Penelope" is a small, rigid heddle table tapestry loom made by Nilus Leclerc. It has a weaving width of twenty-two inches and folds, making it easy to carry and store.

Hem
Selvedge

The woven part of the tapestry that is folded under to form a finished edge.

The edge of the tapestry as it is being woven. The selvedges in tapestry weaving are not always the side edges when the piece is finished, as some tapestries are woven in a side direction (rather than from bottom to top). In such cases, the woven selvedges actually become the top and bottom edges of the tapestry.

GENERAL INSTRUCTIONS

As you proceed through these first few chapters, please read each section until you are asked to stop. After you have completed each portion of the project, return to the text and continue until you reach the next stopping point. General reviews are presented periodically to help you evaluate your progress.

LOOM CONSIDERATIONS

Many kinds of looms are available and most are suitable for tapestry weaving. They range from simple and efficient frame looms and table looms to the more

16.

complex and sophisticated multi-harness floor looms and vertical tapestry looms.

Frame looms usually have rigid heddles that are hand operated, although some are equipped with string heddles. The widths of these looms range from about twenty to thirty-six inches. Most of them have a tension

17.

system and many come with stands that hold the looms, which makes weaving much easier.

Small four-harness table looms use hand levers to raise and lower the harnesses and have some type of tension control. Some small table looms use string heddles while others have rigid heddles or harnesses with hand-operated levers for creating the shed. These looms are usually less expensive than floor looms, and their size and weight make them very portable.

Vertical tapestry looms and floor looms are generally available in widths up to sixty inches, although some professional tapestry looms, both vertical and horizontal, have weaving widths of ten feet or more. These looms are equipped with either harnesses and foot treadles, or string heddles with no harnesses or foot treadles. Both have excellent tension devices that make it possible to keep the warp extremely tight.

Since tapestry is a plain weave technique (see the next section), which requires only two shed combinations, it can be woven on just about any type of loom. However, there are some important points that you should consider. The loom you choose should be sturdy because the warp is wound on very tight, placing considerable strain on the warp as well as the loom. Since a tight warp is very important in tapestry weaving, your loom should also have some sort of tension control that will allow you to tighten the warp during weaving. Be sure that the tension device will hold and not slip when the warp is tightened. If you plan to use a horizontal loom that has harnesses, be sure that the warp can remain perfectly horizontal as it passes from the front of the loom to the back of the loom. Also check that the placement of the heddles in the harnesses does not cause the warp to pull up or down where it passes through the harnesses when the shed is closed.

17. The "Tissart" is a two-harness vertical tapestry loom with foot treadles made by Nilus Leclerc. It is ideal for weaving larger pieces up to sixty inches wide.

18. *The Brittany Anjou tapestry loom is a rigid heddle frame loom with a tension control and adjustable stand that holds the loom in a variety of positions.*

19. *The "Nilus" is a jack-type folding floor loom made by Nilus Leclerc. Widths range from twenty-seven to sixty inches. It is a sturdy four-harness loom with foot treadles.*

20. *In using a loom without a shedding device, as with this nail-frame loom, the shed is created by hand as the fingers pick up every other warp thread. The hands are used to hold the shed open during weaving.*

21. *Opening the shed is quick and easy when using a loom that has foot treadles attached to harnesses.*

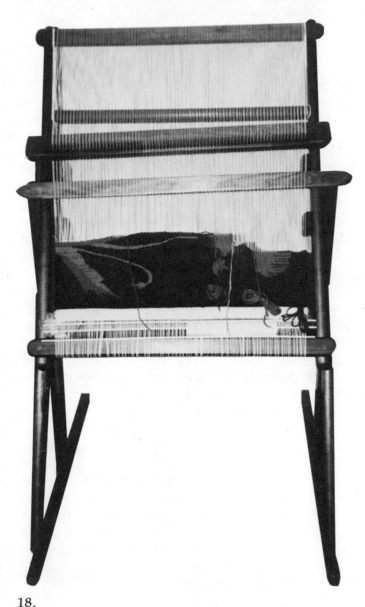

18.

19.

A loom that has some sort of a harness system or shedding device makes it easier to raise the warp threads and weaving progresses more quickly than it does without such devices. However, some people prefer to weave without them, choosing instead to manipulate the shed completely by hand, picking up the warp threads with their fingers (fig. 20). Even though this is somewhat slower, many weavers enjoy the total hand involvement with the weaving materials and therefore prefer this method.

Depending on how much space you have, how much you want to invest in a loom, and how obsessed you become with weaving, you might find you have an overwhelming desire to have more than one loom. Although I weave most of my tapestries on a Leclerc

20.

sixty-inch, four-harness horizontal floor loom, I have four looms, each with a different shedding system. My floor loom allows me to weave more quickly by using harnesses and foot treadles to create the shed (fig. 21). My Brittany Anjou tapestry loom has a rigid heddle bar that is hand operated and uses a batten to hold the shed open (fig. 22). It is convenient to use when weaving smaller pieces, giving weaving demonstrations, and teaching workshops.

My Navajo loom, which I built, offers another type of shedding system, using string heddles fastened around a dowel, and a batten to create the shed (fig. 23). Weaving a Navajo rug on this vertical loom makes me feel close to nature, so it is usually the one I take on camping trips. Sitting there in the peace and quiet of

21.

22.

22. *The Brittany Anjou tapestry loom utilizes a rigid heddle bar and a batten to create the shed.*

23. *A Navajo loom uses string heddles and a batten to create the shed.*

faraway places, I can truly escape into the weaving of the rug.

My small vertical French tapestry loom (fig. 24) is used mainly for weaving color samples, trying new techniques, and experimenting. It is always close by and when I get an inspiration in the middle of weaving another tapestry on a different loom, I try out the idea, while it is still fresh in my mind, on this small loom. It has string heddles, which are fastened around heddle bars and attached to foot treadles.

Each of these looms has its own special feeling and inspires me in a different way. Since you and your loom will become very close, spending many private and fun-filled hours together, choose one that makes you feel good. If you do not have a weaving store in your area that can help you in selecting a loom, refer to the list of loom manufacturers in the "Sources of Weaving Supplies" chapter. Many of them manufacture a variety of looms, including portable frame looms, floor looms, and vertical tapestry looms. If you write to them, I am sure they would be happy to send you a brochure listing the looms they have available.

PLAIN WEAVE

If you have woven before, you might want to skip this section. If not, let's continue.

Tapestry is executed in plain weave, which means that the weft passes over one warp, under the next, over the next, and so on. Through the use of heddles or a shedding device, you can raise every other warp thread, creating the opening that is called the shed. The weft is loosely passed or bubbled through the shed (fig. 25A). The shed is then changed, raising the warp threads that were in the down position on the previous row, and the

23.

weft is passed through this shed in the opposite direction (fig. 25B). Each time the shed is changed, raising the alternate warp threads, the weft passes over the warp threads that it passed under on the previous row.

Bubbling the Weft

The weft is bubbled in order to allow enough yarn to go over and under each warp so that the tapestry will lie flat when the shed is closed. The weft must be loose enough to go over and under each neighboring warp *consistently* without pulling the warp threads together. If you laid the weft in the shed without bubbling it, the edges would draw in, the warp would pull closer and closer together, and pretty soon it would be impossible for the weft to pack down and cover the warp.

WARP CONSIDERATIONS

The warp is the foundation of the tapestry, so be sure to select a good strong warp. Cotton, wool, and linen are the most common types of warp used in tapestry weaving. Cotton has the most elasticity and is therefore easier to control and minor inconsistencies in warping are not as noticeable. I suggest that you use it for your first few tapestries. Wool also has a natural elasticity and is frequently used in weaving rugs, especially those that will actually lie on the floor; there is less wear of materials as they rub against each other if the warp and weft are both wool. Linen is very strong but has little elasticity, which makes it difficult to work with initially, although it gives good results. You might want to try it once you gain some experience in warping your loom.

The color of the warp does not affect the appearance of the finished tapestry because the warp is completely covered by the weft. However, it is easier on

24.

24. *This small vertical tapestry loom uses string heddles fastened around heddle bars, which are attached to foot treadles, to make the shed.*

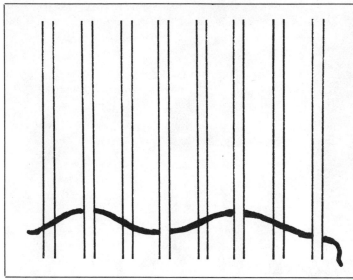

25A.

25. Opening the shed raises every other warp thread. The weft is then loosely passed—or bubbled—through the shed (A). When the shed is changed, the opposite warp threads are raised, and the weft is passed through the shed in the reverse direction (B).

26. This cross section of the warp illustrates the weft passing over and under adjacent warp threads. It is important that the weft be loose enough to go over and under the warp threads consistently.

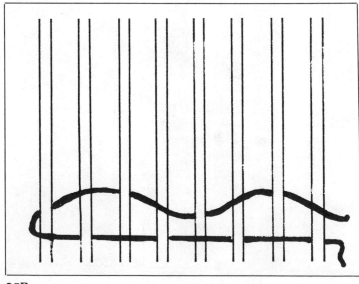

25B.

your eyes while weaving if you use a light color, such as beige or white, rather than a dark shade, especially if you use a cartoon under your warp. If you use a black warp and a cartoon drawn on white paper, the effect will be dazzling—and tiring.

Some kinds of medium and heavy warp that are suitable for tapestry weaving are listed below. These are just a few samples of sizes and can be used as comparisons when selecting other types of warp.

Medium weight:	CUM fishnet twine—size 12/9 or 12/12
	Lily carpet warp—size 8/4
	Lily Frost-Tone—size 10/3
	Cotton twine—size 18
	Lily mercerized cotton—size 3/2
	Linen warp—size 8/5 or 6/3
Heavy weight:	Lily carpet warp—size 3/4
	Cotton twine—size 24
	CUM fishnet twine—size 12/21 or 12/24

Many of these warp sizes are available in most weaving shops. Cotton twine also can be purchased in the hardware section of many stores.

Calculating Warp Quantities

The amount of warp needed for the sample project has, of course, been determined for you, but you will need to learn how to calculate the amount needed for

26.

future projects. However, if this is, at first, a little confusing and if you are weaving your first tapestry, you might want to skip to the next section, "Weft Considerations," and refer back to this section when you calculate the warp for your next tapestry.

To figure how many *yards of warp* are necessary for a project, multiply the *total width* by the number of *warp ends per inch*. Multiply this result by the *length of the warp (in inches)* and divide the result by *thirty-six*.

For example, if you need a *warp length of 68 inches* and the warp is *18 inches wide*, set at *six ends per inch*, you will need *204 yards of warp*. *Allow a little extra width (about one inch) for the warp* when you figure it because the edge will be drawn in slightly as weaving begins. Remember, also, that the finished width of the piece will be slightly narrower when it is removed from the loom than when it was on it. If you are using a double warp at each selvedge, add two extra threads to the total number of warp ends required.

WEFT CONSIDERATIONS

To achieve technical success and weave a good tapestry—one that is consistent; has an even, flat surface (no bumps or ridges); and straight, even edges—you must select your weft yarns carefully. Be sure to use weaving yarns rather than knitting yarns, because weaving yarns are firmer, making them ideal for tapestry weaving. Be aware of different yarn characteristics, such as texture, elasticity, size, and tightness of twist. Each of these has a direct effect on how much the weft must be bubbled during weaving. Lack of knowledge and improper control and handling of the weft, especially when using various types in the same piece, has resulted in many a first tapestry being hung in the closet.

As you begin to select weft yarns for your first few projects, you probably will find it difficult to resist all the different textures, fibers, and sizes, but try to restrain yourself, at least for a little while. I suggest you use wool in the beginning. It is easier to work with because of its natural elasticity, and minor problems concerning edge and surface control can easily be remedied by steaming the tapestry when it is finished.

It will be easier for you to achieve better results in the beginning if you select the same type of weft for your entire tapestry. Each type of yarn has to be handled differently, so if you use wefts with varying amounts of elasticity, it will be necessary to bubble them differently. For example, a yarn that has a lot of elasticity does not have to be bubbled as much as a yarn that has little elasticity.

If it is not possible for you to find all the colors you want in the same yarn, be sure to pick ones that are of equal elasticity and a similar size and weight. Take time to feel the yarn and look at it closely. Check the label and compare the number of yards per ounce. To check the elasticity, give a short piece a little tug and see how much it stretches.

After you have a little weaving experience and feel comfortable with the techniques as well as with control of yarns, try some handspun yarns. They create a totally different and exciting look. You can create interesting shading by carding or spinning two shades of wool together, and even more creative combinations if you dye your own handspun (see the "Some Fun with Handspun" section in the "A Quick Review . . . " chapter).

If you do not spin, you can purchase handspun in many weaving shops. Also, your local weavers' guild might be able to tell you of someone who sells handspun yarn. (If you would like to learn to spin, see the "Further

menting with different yarns, be sure to take detailed notes. It will be very helpful when calculating weft quantities later on to know how many yards per ounce or skein a particular yarn contains and how many rows of that weft it takes to weave an inch. You will be surprised how quickly these little details fade from memory and how necessary your notes will be.

You will spend many enjoyable hours selecting just the right size, texture, and color of weft for your tapestries. Here are a few wefts that are available in different sizes and are found in most weaving stores:

Tahki yarns—fine, medium, and heavy
CUM Asborya—medium
CUM Mattgarn—medium
CUM Swedish wool 7/2 two ply—fine
CUM Gobelin-Broderigarn—fine
Paternayan crewel yarns—fine
Paternayan Persian yarns—medium
Mexican homespun—medium and heavy
Condon's Canadian wool yarns two and three ply—medium—and five ply—heavy
Briggs & Little Woolen Mills two ply—medium
Manos of Uruguay—medium and heavy
Craft Yarns/Persian—medium
Berber wools—medium and heavy
Grandor yarns—medium and heavy
Mill ends—come on cones in all sizes

Choosing colors can sometimes be confusing. If you find it difficult to imagine how two colors are going to look when woven side by side, simply take a strand of each and twist them loosely together. This will give you a good idea of their compatibility. I also get a better feel for color when the yarn has been wound into balls. The smooth surface gives a truer representation of how the color will look when woven. Therefore, before I

27. A Saxony spinning wheel from Finland is displayed here with carded fleeces and the finished product—handspun yarns. Using handspun in tapestries offers interesting and unusual results.

27.

Reading" chapter.)

As you continue to experiment with tapestry weaving, you might want to try using some different kinds of weft fibers, such as cotton, linen, and silk. All of these work nicely with wool weft, and successfully combining them will challenge you further. As you start experi-

begin weaving I wind all skeins into balls (fig. 28) and place them on a shelf close to the loom. This makes it convenient to wind bobbins or butterflies quickly, and anytime I need to check color combinations, I can easily twist the colors together.

Calculating Weft Quantities

As with the warp, the quantities of weft needed for the project in this book have been figured for you, but eventually you will have to do it yourself. Determining an accurate amount of weft is a little more difficult than determining the amount of warp. You have to combine a mathematical calculation with an educated guess. If you are weaving your first tapestry, you might want to skip this information and go on to the next section, "Tips," and refer back to this section when you start your next piece.

You can get a fairly realistic figure of the number of

28.

28. *A ball winder* (left) *and a skein winder* (right) *are used to wind skeins of weft into balls. Having the yarn in balls can make it easier to determine what effect the colors will have when woven.*

yards of weft needed for each design area by multiplying the *width of the area* by the *height*, then multiplying the result by the *number of rows of weft woven per inch* and dividing by *thirty-six*.

For example, if the area is *three inches wide* and *four inches high* and you pack this particular weft at about *twenty-five rows per inch*, you will need about *eight and one-third yards of weft. Be sure to allow a little extra for bubbling each row.* You will have to estimate this amount based on your own experience, and rely on your note taking. Just keep in mind that it is better to have a little extra on hand than to run out in the middle of the tapestry and learn that the color you need is out of stock or that it has been discontinued.

Tips

Regardless of the wefts you choose to use in the future, remember the following:

1. The less elasticity the yarn has, the more it is bubbled during weaving.
2. The greater the elasticity, the less it is bubbled.
3. More tightly twisted yarns must be bubbled more than more loosely spun yarns.
4. Thicker yarns must be bubbled more than finer yarns.
5. Handspun must be bubbled a little more than commercially spun yarns.
6. Blocked handspun—in which the twist has been set by washing and blocking—achieves a more uniform result and is easier to control initially than unblocked handspun.
7. Unblocked handspun can add wonderful texture to a tapestry but requires a different amount of bubbling than blocked handspun.

This amount will vary depending on how tight the yarn is spun, so you may have to do some experimenting.

THE WARP-WEFT RELATIONSHIP

Two of the questions most frequently asked by beginning tapestry weavers are: "How do I know what size weft to use?" and "How wide do I space the warp?" A good general rule is that the size of the weft should fit in the space between two warp threads (fig. 29). If you are using a loom that allows you to get the warp extremely tight, the weft can be a little wider and it will still pack close enough to cover the warp. If the weft is too thick and heavy, you will not be able to pack the weft tight enough to cover the warp.

The warp-weft relationship should be considered as it will vary the overall appearance of your piece. For the sake of simplicity, the following examples refer to only two sizes of warp—medium and heavy—and three sizes of weft—fine, medium, and heavy. The weft can be a single strand or multiple strands. (For more information about multiple strands, see the "Additional Tapestry Techniques" section of the "A Quick Review . . ." chapter.)

To determine how wide to space your warp, consider the size of the warp, the size of the weft, the intricacy of the design, and the feel you want the tapestry to have. Do you want it thick, coarse in texture, medium weight or very fine? Because the warp and weft are usually at right angles to one another, a little stair-step effect occurs every time the design moves over a warp. If the design is very intricate, you will want to space the warp closer together than might be necessary for a less detailed piece. The design will be easier to weave, the lines will flow better, and the stair-step effect will be less noticeable. This is especially true when weaving small curves and circles. Since warp and weft are at right angles to one another, the edges of curves and circles are made up of little straight lines. In order to give the shape a rounded appearance, the warp must be closer together.

The following will give you a feel for various combinations:

1. For a coarse weave, try a medium-weight warp spaced at about four to five ends per inch, and use a heavy-weight weft.
2. For a thick weave (one that actually increases the thickness of the piece and is more dense than a coarse weave), try a heavy-weight warp spaced at four to five ends per inch, and use a medium-weight weft.
3. For a medium-weight piece, set a medium-weight warp at about six to eight ends per inch, and use a medium-weight weft.
4. For a fine texture, set a medium-weight warp at about ten to twelve ends per inch, and use a fine-weight weft.

This whole idea of the warp-weft relationship relates directly to the space between warp threads. For example, in comparing items one and two in the preceding list, you can see that if you set a medium and

29. *A general guideline for selecting the proper weft size is that the weft should fit in the space between warp threads.*

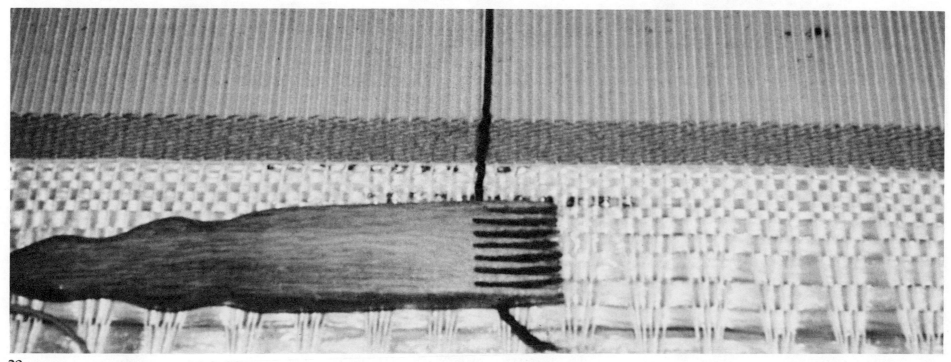

29.

30.

heavy warp at the same number of ends per inch, the space created between the warp threads would be different. The heavier warp takes up more space, therefore leaving less space between warp threads, and requires a smaller-sized weft than the medium-sized warp.

Remember that these are just some guidelines to make you aware of various combinations and the effects they produce. You might also find that it is easier to use a little smaller weft (in these combinations) when you are packing with the beater on your loom instead of hand packing with a fork.

If you space the warp too close for the size of the weft and find that you actually have to "beat" it hard, forcing it to cover the warp, the results might be somewhat different from what you anticipated. A friend who used a weft that was too heavy had that feeling of "Oh, maybe it will be okay," and continued weaving. As she forced the weft to cover the warp, packing it very hard, the piece rippled in some places. When she removed the piece from the loom, the ripples flattened out, causing the piece to widen, which distorted the image. Since the image in the tapestry was a face, I asked her if she was disappointed with the results. Actually, she was pleasantly surprised, feeling that it created an interesting effect, as you can see in figure 30. If this brings all kinds of wild visions to mind, you might want to try this intentionally and see what kind of special effects you can create.

The instructions for the sample tapestry you will be weaving suggest that you use a medium-weight warp (such as the ones listed previously in the "Warp Considerations" section) set at six ends per inch, and a medium-weight weft (listed in the "Weft Considerations" section). Using this combination, the weft will pack and cover the warp nicely at about twenty-five rows per inch.

Tips

1. If you choose a weft that is too heavy or tightly spun for the setting of the warp, it will not pack down evenly and may not completely cover the warp.
2. If the weft is too fine, it will take many more rows of weaving and use a lot more yarn than if it were a little heavier weight.
3. The larger the weft, the wider you space the warp.
4. The finer the weft, the closer you space the warp.

30. *"Amy" was woven on a frame loom with a cotton warp set at twelve ends per inch. It was warped with too close a set for the diameter of the weft, so vertical ripples occurred while the piece was on the loom. The selvedges were straight, however, and off the loom the piece spread at the top and the ripples disappeared, leaving the piece with an interesting distorted image. The weft is handspun wool, dog hair, and silk. (Woven by Sylvia Tessore of Sacramento, California)*

3

GETTING READY TO WEAVE

T HE SAMPLE PROJECT
 Before you can begin any tapestry, you need to consider many questions. After deciding on the design and selecting the weft yarns, you will need to decide in which direction the tapestry should be woven. Should you weave it from bottom to top or from side to side? Let the design help you. It is easier to weave horizontal lines than vertical lines and the curves and angles, if horizontal, are more successfully woven. Looking at the design for the sample project in figure 31, you can see that it will be easier to weave it from bottom to top as there are fewer vertical lines in that direction. Consider the total piece. Some of these things might influence the design as well as the loom you choose to use:

1. Will you weave the piece with the right side facing you as you weave or will you weave it with the back side facing you? If you weave with the back side facing you, your cartoon will have to be drawn in reverse, being a mirror image of the piece.
2. How will you finish the bottom and top edge? Will these become the sides of the tapestry when it is hung on the wall?
3. Do you want fringe? Will you weave it in or add it later?
4. How will the finished piece be mounted?
5. How heavy will the tapestry be? Will your rod or other mounting device support the piece properly and display it nicely?

Answers to all these questions will be given as you work on the sample tapestry. The instructions for this project will guide you, step by step, through the various stages involved in the preparation and weaving of a tapestry. As you work on the project, think about each step and solution, because you will be making all these decisions when you start your next piece. Remember always to plan ahead, keeping in mind the total tapestry.

For this sample tapestry, you will weave using the building-up technique, weaving a design area at a time. The weaving will progress from bottom to top with the right side facing you as you work. The cartoon is a black-and-white outline and the design areas are numbered. Select the colors you want for each area in the quantities listed in the next section, "Materials Needed." The colors listed next to the numbers and letters are those used by the student who wove the sample shown in figure 32. Feel free to select your own color combina-

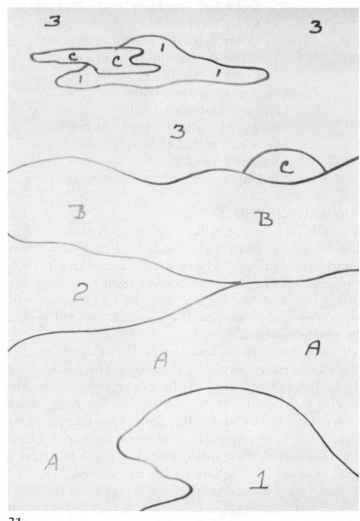

31.

32.

31. *It is best to weave the sample project from bottom to top because the design has so many horizontal lines. (Turning the cartoon and weaving the design sideways would make the horizontal lines become vertical lines, and vertical design lines are more difficult to weave.)*

32. *The sample project looks something like this when finished, depending on what yarns are chosen. Unevenly dyed yarn created the random shading in the area at the top. The tapestry shown here is larger than the sample project.*

tions to make a pleasing landscape scene. After selecting your weft yarns, you might want to label them to correspond with the area where they will be used.

This project is designed with the beginner in mind.

It includes large areas and soft curving lines, allowing you to concentrate on yarn control, edge and surface control, and basic techniques. In some areas, the design runs from edge to edge. In other areas, many different wefts are used to make up the total width of the piece. This allows you to experiment with the amount of bubbling necessary to keep the width of the piece the same as weaving progresses from an area where several wefts are used to areas where a single weft is used. As the project continues, it becomes a little more challenging because of the small half-circle and some smaller design areas.

MATERIALS NEEDED
    Pencil
    Ruler
    Piece of paper, twelve by twenty inches
    Loom with a width of at least thirteen inches that can accommodate a finished length of nineteen inches; it should also have some sort of a shedding device or heddle system
    Scissors
    T-pins (to pin the cartoon to the warp)
    Yardstick
    Heading material (plastic strips) at least sixteen inches long
    Fork or comb for packing. (In using the building-up technique, you cannot use the beater on the loom, if your loom has one.)
    About 175 yards of medium-weight cotton warp (see "Warp Considerations" section in preceding chapter)
    Weft (amounts based on packing the weft at twenty-five to thirty rows per inch). Remember, it is easier initially if you select yarns of a similar size and elasticity (see "Weft Considerations" section in preceding chapter):
        Color one (dark rust)—75 yards
        Color two (medium rust)—25 yards
        Color three (light rust)—100 yards
        Color A (dark brown)—100 yards
        Color B (medium brown)—65 yards
        Color C (gold)—10 yards
    Finishing and mounting materials:
        Large-eyed tapestry needle
        One board, ¼ by ¾ by 13 inches long
        Staple gun and staples (or tacks)
        Two small nails
        Sandpaper

ENLARGING THE DESIGN
    The cartoon you will be enlarging is shown in figure 33, and is three inches wide and four and three-quarters inches high. I have drawn a grid in half-inch squares over the design. Since we want to enlarge the design to four times this size, each half-inch square will equal two inches, making the full-scale cartoon twelve by nineteen inches.

    The first step in transferring the image is to grid your large paper. Begin by drawing a line one inch up from the bottom edge of the paper clear across the twelve-inch width. Then, starting at one edge, mark every two inches along this line. Continue marking every two inches around all edges of the paper. Draw lines connecting these marks and your paper will have a grid in which each square equals two inches.

    An easy way to transfer the image from the small design to the large paper is to mark dots at key points at the appropriate measurements on your enlargement. Many of these key points have been marked with an X in a circle to help you get started. For example, the rightmost line of design area one is at the first grid mark. Remember, each half-inch equals two inches on the enlargement. Mark a dot at the two-inch mark along the right edge of your enlargement. The topmost point of design area one is seven inches from the left edge and five and one-half inches from the bottom. Continue marking dots at these key points. As you complete an area, draw connecting lines between dots, referring to the original. Try to capture curves and angles as closely as possible.

This simple grid technique allows you to enlarge a design to any size and still keep the entire design in proper proportion. One-quarter inch might equal an inch on the enlargement or one inch could equal one foot. I know you will find this enlargement technique very helpful as you experiment with various designing techniques. Stop now and enlarge the sample design into a full-scale cartoon and transfer the letter and number codes to their respective design areas.

TIME TO WARP

You are now ready to warp the loom, but before you do, read this section completely. (For specific instructions on how to warp your loom, please refer to the instructions that come with it.)

This project requires a warp length of nineteen inches. Be sure to allow enough additional length to tie on or wrap around your loom, depending on the kind of loom you have. If you are using a four-harness loom, it is necessary to use only two of the harnesses when weaving a tapestry. However, you can use four if you like, threading them one, two, three, and four, and tying harness one and three to one foot treadle and harness two and four to another foot treadle.

Set the warp at six ends per inch for a width of thirteen inches. If the width of your loom is wider than thirteen inches, be sure to center the warp on the loom. Since my loom has a reed, I use a twelve-dent reed when

setting my warp at six ends per inch, threading the warp through every other dent. This smaller-spaced reed helps hold the warp in place better than a six-dent reed,

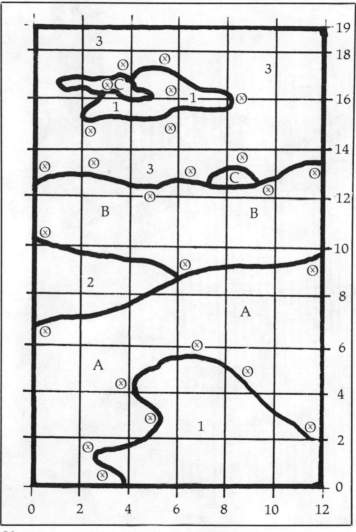

33. To enlarge a design, grid the original and transfer the image, area by area, to the full-scale paper.

33.

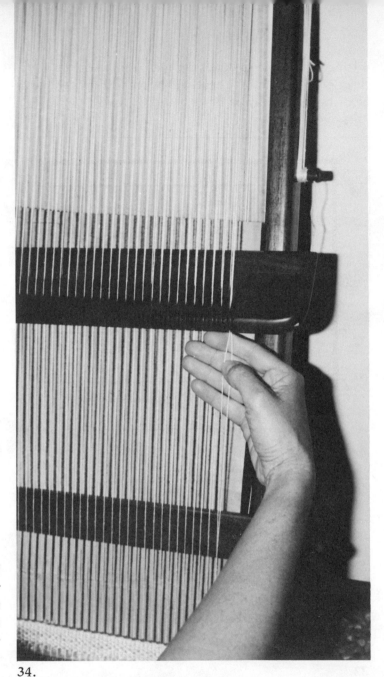

which would allow the warp to move from side to side in the dent. It is important to keep the warp as close to perpendicular as possible and to keep it from moving sideways. This would cause inconsistent spacing in the warp, which would result in ridges forming on the surface of the tapestry.

Using a double instead of a single warp at each selvedge is a technique I like to use because it makes a firm, even edge. This double warp is treated as a single warp when weaving. If you are using a loom with harnesses and heddles, pass these two edge warps through the same dent in the reed and through separate heddles on the same harness. If you are using a rigid heddle loom, thread these two warp threads through the same slot (fig. 34).

If you are using a loom with a continuous warp (one in which the warp is wrapped around the loom—see fig. 35), try to set aside enough time to complete the process in one sitting. You will be able to get a more even, consistent tension on all warp threads if you do it all at one time. If, despite your efforts, the warp has a loose area, you can adjust it. Starting at that area, gently pull on the warp, taking up the slack in each warp as you work toward the edge, then retie the knot that securely holds the warp at the edge.

If you are using a loom that requires that the warp be tied on rather than wrapped around, be sure to tie it on in small groups of approximately six ends (fig. 36). If you tie it on in large groups, all those warp threads in the center of each group will be looser than the ones on the edge of each group. The larger the group the worse the problem. And believe me, those soft areas in the warp will haunt you during weaving and cause nothing but trouble. If you have a long warp on the loom, the problems will seem to get worse as you go.

34. With a rigid heddle loom, two warp threads are threaded through the same slot in order to have a double warp at each edge. This edge warp is treated as a single warp during the weaving process.

34.

After you have warped your loom very consistently, tighten the warp so it is very snug. "How snug is tight enough?" The tighter the warp the better. I tighten my warp as tightly as my loom will allow and still have it be possible to open the shed. You do not need a large shed

36.

35.

opening since you can open it farther with your hands as you pass the weft through the individual design areas. If you are accustomed to weaving fabric (as I was), what you might think is a nice snug warp is actually soft compared with what is required for tapestry weaving. *Remember, the warp is the foundation of your tapestry and is, in my mind, the single most important factor in weaving a technically successful piece—one with straight, even edges and a flat, smooth surface.*

Tips

1. A tight warp helps eliminate uneven edges during weaving.
2. A tight warp allows the weft to pack down evenly and easily.

35. *The warp is wound around a loom that has a continuous warp. The tension of the warp will be more consistent if it is wound on at one time rather than in separate sittings.*

36. *On a loom in which the warp is tied on, a more consistent warp is achieved if the warp is tied in small groups of about six ends.*

3. A tight warp helps keep the warp threads perpendicular and in place.
4. A double warp at each selvedge adds strength and evenness to the piece.
5. Tying the warp in small groups eliminates soft areas.
6. Being sure the warp tension is tight and consistent—feeling it carefully and being critical—will save you a lot of regrets later on.

Keeping these hints in mind, stop now and warp your loom, then proceed to the next section, "Knowing Your Loom."

KNOWING YOUR LOOM

If you have never woven on your loom, take time now to get acquainted with it. Can you open the shed easily and change it quickly? Practice a few times. Do you know how to advance the warp? After you weave a few inches, it will be necessary to move the warp forward, which keeps the weaving area directly in front of you. Review your loom instructions for the proper procedure. Be sure that the warp tension is even across the entire width of the loom. This is the last chance to adjust it before weaving begins.

THE HEADING

The heading spaces the warp threads evenly and creates a firm, even edge against which to weave. You may use plastic bags cut into strips, heavy yarn, or rags; the heading will be removed when the tapestry is completed.

For the sake of clarity in this project, you will always weave from right to left in shed one (the first shed opened), and from left to right in shed two (the opposite shed). If you have woven before, please stop now and weave a two-inch heading and then proceed to the next section, "Securing Warp Ends." Otherwise, please continue with the detailed instructions until you are asked to stop.

Keep in mind that if you are using your fingers to create the shed, you will pick up the odd-numbered warp threads (one, three, five, and so on) to create the first shed and the even-numbered warp threads (two, four, six, and so on) to create the second shed. Now let's get started weaving:

1. Open the shed (think of this as shed one) and pass the plastic strip (or other heading material) from *right to left*, bubbling it across the row. Pack it in place with your fork (fig. 37A) in the direction it was woven (right to left).
2. Change the shed (this will be shed two) and pass another piece of heading material from *left to right*, packing it in place in a left to right direction (fig. 37B). *Tip:* Always packing in the direction the weft is traveling will help you get a smooth surface on your tapestry. This procedure helps pull in the proper amount of weft needed to cover the warp on each row adequately.
3. Continue weaving rows of heading in this manner for approximately two inches or until all warp threads are evenly spaced.

Be sure that the heading is straight across the entire width. This is the base of your tapestry and if it is not even, your tapestry will be uneven along the bottom edge, which could result in its not hanging straight when it is finished.

Stop now and weave the heading until all warp threads are evenly spaced, working from right to left in shed one and from left to right in shed two.

SECURING WARP ENDS

Now that you have the warp threads evenly spaced, keep an eye on them as you continue to weave. If they do not stay evenly spaced, ridges will appear on the surface of your tapestry as the warp spacing widens or narrows. In addition, if groups of warp threads start to pull together, the weft will not pack down in that area and will not cover the warp. In areas where warp threads pull farther apart, the weft will pack down too tight, causing low areas.

The warp threads must be fastened in some manner, either before or after weaving the piece, in order to prevent the tapestry from unweaving. The person who introduced me to tapestry weaving shared a technique with me that I have used ever since, finding it quick, easy, and effective. By tying double half-hitches around each *pair* of warp threads, just above the heading, the warp ends cannot work loose when the piece is removed from the loom (fig. 38).

This is how it's done. (Please read through the entire explanation before you begin.) Measure an extra piece of warp thread that is about three times the width of the weaving. (You will need a piece that is thirty-six inches long for this project.) Wind it up so it is a manageable length. Do *not* open the shed.

Start at the left side of the warp. Pick up the first

37A.

37B.

37. A heading is woven to space the warp threads evenly. Row one is woven, then packed, in a right to left direction (A). The second row, woven in the opposite shed, is woven from left to right and is packed in a left to right direction (B).

38.

38. *Warp ends can be secured by tying double half-hitches around each warp pair.*

39. *A separate warp strand travels under and around warp pairs, circling them twice, to form double half-hitches.*

40. *A triple half-hitch is necessary to secure each edge warp pair.*

pair of warp threads (remember, the double warp at the edge is treated as a single warp) and pass the strand of warp thread under the pair of warp threads in a right to left direction, leaving a short end extending on the surface at the right of the pair. Circle the warp pair again, always going under the right side of the pair. As you bring the warp strand across the pair, pass it through the loop that was created by the circling (fig. 39) and pull until it is snug. Each time you go around the pair of warp threads and through the loop, you will have completed a half hitch. It is necessary to go around each pair twice to create a double half-hitch. Pulling straight down helps keep the warp threads perpendicular. When you start, go around the *edge* pair three times (fig. 40), then move to the next pair to the right, tying a double half-hitch around each pair. Continue across the entire width, a pair at a time. When you reach the right edge, be sure to make three half hitches around this pair.

If you start at the right edge, you will be going under the pairs of warp threads in a left to right direction and you will work around each pair, moving toward the left edge.

This is my favorite way to secure the warp ends; however, I have suggested alternate methods in the "Securing Warp Ends" section of the "Finishing, Mounting, and Tapestry Care" chapter.

Stop now and tightly secure the warp ends with double half-hitches, being sure that the pairs stay evenly spaced (fig. 41).

WINDING BUTTERFLIES

Although bobbins, shuttles, and butterflies can be used to pass the weft through the shed, you might find it easier to use butterflies for this small sample project. If you already know how to wind butterflies, please wind several of colors one and A and then skip to the next sec-

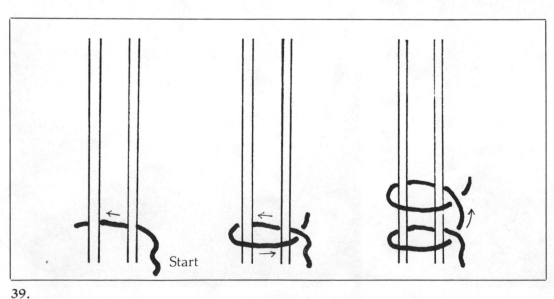

39.

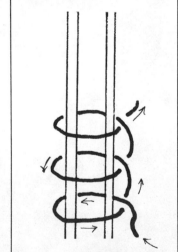

40.

tion, "The Hem."

This small skein of weft is prepared as follows. Take one end of the weft yarn and place it between the middle and ring finger of either hand, leaving an end extending. Bring the yarn across your palm and behind your thumb, cross over the palm again, and go around behind your little finger (fig. 42). Bring the yarn across the palm again and back around your thumb. Continue this figure-eight motion ten to fifteen times. *Do not make the butterfly too large.* If you do, it will not pass through the shed easily and will tend to get all tangled up. Break the yarn, slip the butterfly from your hand, holding it in the center, and wind this finishing end around the center several times. When you get to the last revolution, leave it loose and slip the end through the loop, securing it by pulling until it is snug.

To use it, simply pull gently on the end that you left free when you started preparing the butterfly.

Stop now and wind several butterflies of colors one and A.

THE HEM

Weaving a one-inch hem provides a nice finish for the lower edge of the tapestry. When I weave a tapestry with a heavy weft, I use a smaller-sized weft for the hem. This makes it fold under smoothly and is especially nice when the tapestry is woven sideways and these hemmed edges become the side edges when the tapestry is hung on the wall.

When weaving the hem, the weft travels from edge to edge. You thus should bubble the weft a little more than when you are weaving the individual design areas, in which the weft travels back and forth within only a specific design area. The basic weaving process presented here is the procedure used for weaving in

general and will be used throughout your project. The knowledgeable weaver may want to skip to the next section, "Joining a New Weft."

Please read through the entire set of instructions and through the section "Tips," then review the illustrations until you are asked to stop.

With a butterfly of color one, start at the right edge:

1. Open shed one and pass the weft from right to left, leaving a short end—about one inch—extending at the right edge. Lay the weft in loose, bubbling it *consistently* across the row (fig. 43A).
2. Pack it in place with a fork in the direction the weft travels. This is row one.
3. Change the shed and pass the weft from left to right, again bubbling consistently across the row (fig. 43B). The end that was left extend-

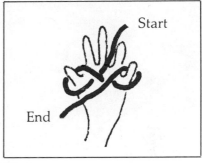

42.

41. *The pairs of warp threads must stay evenly spaced as the double half-hitches are tied across the entire width.*

42. *A butterfly is formed by winding the yarn in a figure-eight fashion around the fingers.*

41.

43A.

43B.

43. In weaving the hem, row one travels from right to left and is bubbled consistently (A). After row one is packed in place, row two of the hem passes in the opposite direction of row one, and again is bubbled and packed in place (B).

44. One way to join wefts is to overlap them over two warp threads, leaving the ends extending on the back side of the tapestry.

ing on row one should be tucked in on row two. Bring the end back in the row (as you start row two) and over two warp ends, then tuck the loose end through to the back of the tapestry. Pack the weft in place.

4. Change the shed and continue, repeating this sequence.

Joining a New Weft

When you finish one butterfly and start with another, there are several ways to make the join. You can tuck the end through the warp to the back side of the tapestry, overlap the new piece of weft (two warp threads), and tuck the end of the new piece of weft to the back. Leave an end of about one inch extending out the back (fig. 44).

For the sake of simplicity, the remaining illustra-

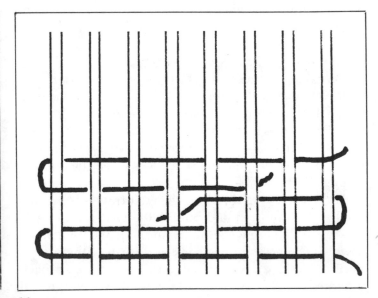

44.

tions of weft and warp will not show the weft being bubbled on each row but will show only the placement of weft over and under the warp. *As you weave, remember to bubble the weft.*

It is not necessary to overlap the wefts at the point where they join. You can simply push the ends of the old and the new wefts through to the back of the tapestry, right next to each other (fig. 45).

If you are using a wool weft, which will fray when broken, use the Navajo technique of weaving in the ends. Break the end of the weft and leave it in the shed. Break the end of the new weft and overlap this frayed end with the other frayed weft end and pack them in place (fig. 46). Do not cut the weft or you will not get the frayed end, which is what makes this technique work so nicely. When joining wefts this way, the back side of the tapestry will look as finished as the front side.

Tips

1. Make the bubbles the same size across each row and do not push them down through the warp.
2. Push the point of the bubble close to the previous weaving line but not so close that a loop appears on the surface when the weft is packed in place.
3. To help keep the edges straight, hold the weft in place as it wraps around the edge warp (fig. 47). Be careful to grasp only one or two warp threads. If you hold the weft in place around five or six warp threads, they will gradually pull together because the weft has not been bubbled in that area.

Stop now and weave a one-inch hem using color one, finishing with the weft at the right edge.

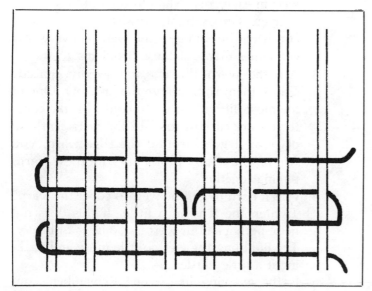

45.

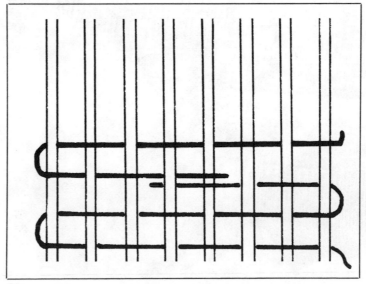

46.

45. *In joining wefts, the ends do not have to be overlapped but can just extend to the back side.*

46. *With a wool weft, ends can be frayed and overlapped in the shed. Because this leaves no loose ends, the tapestry looks as finished on the back side as on the front.*

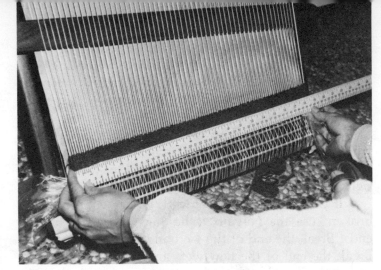

EVALUATING YOUR TECHNIQUE

Now that you have woven the hem, let's take a few minutes to look at it.

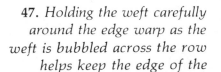

47. Holding the weft carefully around the edge warp as the weft is bubbled across the row helps keep the edge of the tapestry straight.

48. After weaving the hem, measure the width with a yardstick.

1. Are there any bumps of weft on the surface? If so, you probably pushed the weft too close to the previous weaving line. You may also have bubbled the weft too much.

2. Is the width the same at the beginning of the hem as it is at the end? Measure it carefully (fig. 48), using a yardstick rather than a tape measure. (Because a tape measure has give and can be stretched when pulled too tight, it

48.

can show an incorrect measurement.) If the edge draws in, you are not bubbling the weft enough on each row. You might want to tighten the warp a little, also. If the width begins to get wider, you are putting too much weft in each row. Make those bubbles a little smaller. *Tip:* A tight, consistent tension and consistent bubbling of the weft on every row eliminates many of these problems.

3. Are the warp threads still evenly spaced? Check them right above the last row. One of the most difficult areas to control is the edge. If you are careful to hold the weft gently in place as it goes around the edge warp, you will not have any problems with these warps pulling together.

4. Was it hard to get the weft to cover the warp? Tighten the tension a little. If this does not help, perhaps your weft is too large or heavy. Try bubbling the weft a little more and packing it a little harder.

5. Is the weaving line even? Remember, con-

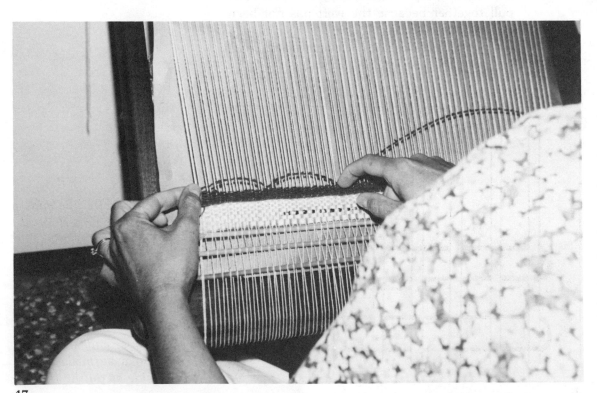

47.

sistency counts. If your warp is tight, your bubbling is consistent across each row, and it is packed evenly, you will not have any trouble. Practice good techniques from the beginning. Soon they will become automatic and you will be pleased with your success.

6. How many rows of weft did it take you to weave the one-inch hem? Just count the number of times the weft circles the edge warp (fig. 49). If you count ten, you are weaving twenty rows per inch. Did you count fifteen? Then you are weaving thirty rows per inch.

It is easy for the beginning tapestry weaver to overpack the weft. You do not need to pack it hard. If your tension is tight, the weft will pack down firm without much effort. Always pack in the direction the weft is traveling as this prevents loops from appearing at the edge, keeps the warp spacing under control, and prevents ridges from forming on the surface of the tapestry. *Ridges are caused by putting more weft in one row than the next.*

ADDING FRINGE DURING WEAVING

Traditionally, tapestries do not have fringe. However, since you are weaving this tapestry from bottom to top, you can add fringe if you want to during this part of the weaving process by tying rya knots around pairs of warp threads.

To do this you will need to cut strands of weft twice the length of the finished fringe. If you want the fringe to be four inches in length, select a book or piece of cardboard that is four inches wide. Wind some weft yarn around this object until you have the number of strands of weft needed for the fringe. For a fuller fringe, you may want to use several strands of yarn in each rya

knot. Using two strands in each knot, you will need approximately seventy-eight pieces for this project. After winding all the yarn, remove it from the book or cardboard by cutting it across one end only. Each strand will be eight inches long.

Rya knots are tied around two warp threads. Do not open the shed. Place the fringe yarn over the top of the two warp threads, bring each end around and up between the two warp threads, and pull until they are snug. You do not actually tie a knot—this looping process forms the rya knot. Start at one edge and tie rya knots across the width of the tapestry just above the woven hem. You will get a nicer finish at each edge if you tie the fringe around three warp threads instead of two (fig. 50). After you have added all the fringe, firmly pack it against the hem.

THE WEAVING SEQUENCE

When weaving a tapestry a design area at a time (which you will be doing for this project), always start

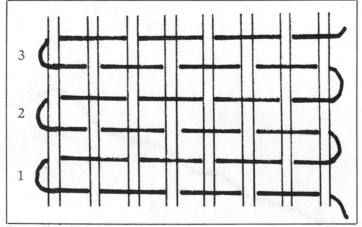

49.

49. *To determine how many rows it takes to weave an inch, double the number of times the weft goes around the edge warp. Keeping track of this information for each kind of yarn you use will be valuable when you calculate weft quantities in future projects.*

by weaving the area that will be the foundation for the adjoining area. In other words, the design area that is decreasing in size at any given point must be woven before the adjoining area can be woven. For example, to weave the design in figure 51, weave area A before area B. As you can see, area B "rests" on area A, therefore A must be woven first.

To weave the design in figure 52, weave area A first, then area B, then areas C and D. If the areas were quite large, you would weave part of A, part of B (bringing the weaving line up even), then finish A and B before weaving C and D.

To weave a circle (fig. 53), the areas below and around the circle, up to the midpoint of the circle, are woven first. Begin by weaving the area below the circle, then the areas to the left and right of the circle, up to the center of the circle. Weave the entire circle next and finish by weaving the remaining areas to the left and right, and above the circle, as indicated by the

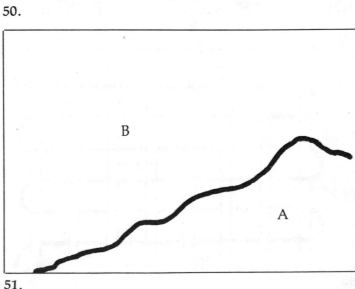

50. *Using rya knots is a good way to add fringe during weaving. Separate strands of weft are tied around pairs of warp threads.*

50.

51. *Because area B rests on area A, area A must be woven first.*

52. *Always weave the decreasing area first, building a foundation for the adjoining area. In this design, the areas would be woven according to the lettered sequence.*

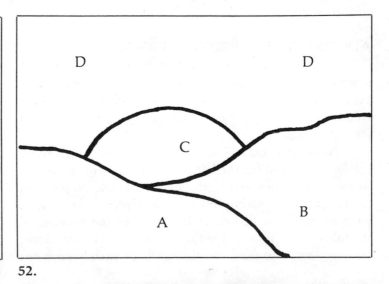

51.

52.

numbered sequence.

A circle is one of the most difficult shapes to weave. Its bottom, sides, and top are actually straight lines. As its size increases, a stair-step effect forms as you move the weft from warp to warp. As the circle gets larger, you weave more rows before moving the weft to the next warp. You will get a rounder edge if you increase the number of rows woven around each warp in a consistent sequence until the straight side edge of the circle is reached. This side area takes the most rows of weft.

For example, after weaving the area below the circle in figure 54, you weave only one pass around warp ten to weave the area to the right of the circle. As the curve moves to warp eleven, two passes are needed. As the circle continues to widen, three passes are needed around warp twelve, three passes around warp thirteen, five passes around warp fourteen, seven around warp fifteen, eleven around warp sixteen, and nineteen passes around warp seventeen, the straight edge of the circle.

You will notice that each time the weft moves over a warp that at least the same number of rows are woven, never fewer. It is this consistently increasing number of woven rows that is the key to success in achieving a well-rounded circle. When the top half of the circle is woven, as the shape starts to decrease, this sequence used for the lower half of the circle is repeated in the reverse sequence.

Depending on the size of the weft, the spacing of the warp, and the size of the circle, the number of rows needed to create the circle will vary.

When weaving large design areas or areas that travel the entire width of the tapestry, the edge of the tapestry may draw in a little at these larger areas. To overcome this problem, weave the area as though you were weaving two (or more) separate design areas in the same color.

For example, in figure 55A design areas one and five are broken in half. The first half of the area is woven by moving over one warp (decreasing) each time you turn around a warp and change the direction of the row. After weaving for an inch or so, you weave the other half of this area, moving the weft over one warp (increasing) on each row (fig. 55B). This is referred to as a lazy line because a slight line is visible where the two areas join. Since you are working with the same color,

use lazy lines

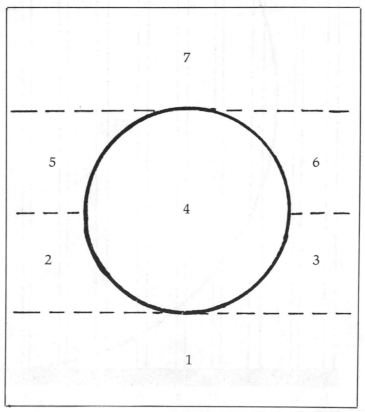

53.

53. *This numbered sequence is followed when weaving a circle. First, the area below and to each side (up to the center) of the circle is woven. Then the circle is woven. Next the areas to the left, right, and above the circle are woven.*

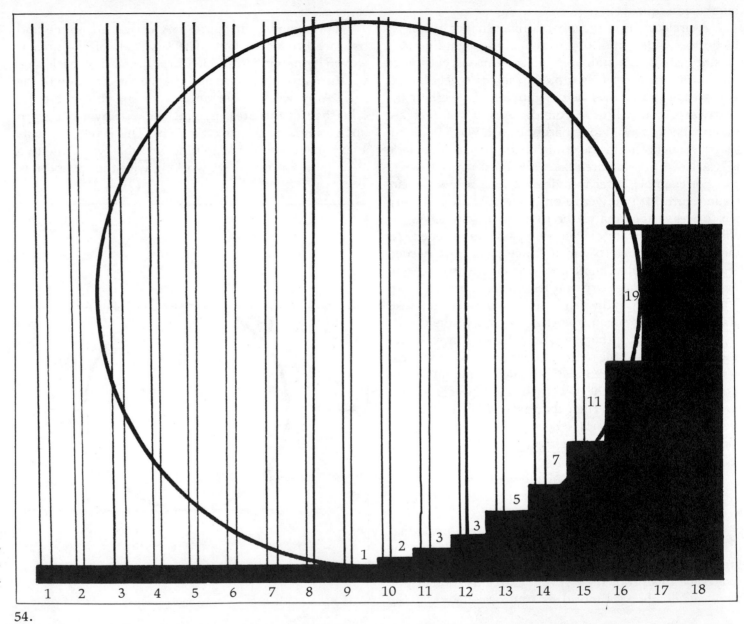

54. *As the circle gets wider, the angle gets steeper, so more rows are woven each time the weft moves over to the next warp.*

54.

the line is barely visible. Other ways to weave a lazy line are included in the "Additional Tapestry Techniques" section of the "A Quick Review..." chapter.

These larger design areas require more weft than smaller areas do. (This helps keep the width of the tapestry even.) Therefore, bubble the weft a little more in large design areas and a little less in small design areas. If you bubble the weft as much in a small area as you do in a large one, the small area will have too much weft and that part of the tapestry will buckle when removed from the loom. That area of the weaving will also be wider than the rest. *I cannot emphasize enough the importance of being aware of the following: the size of the design area, the type and size of the weft, and what effect they have on the amount of bubbling that is necessary to keep the surface flat and the edges straight when the piece is removed from the loom.* If you have only three or four design areas in one part of the weaving and the next section is made up of twenty individual areas, bubbling must be less in these smaller areas than it was in the larger ones.

Tips

1. Weaving continues in a design area until the direction of the design changes.
2. Remember to bring the weaving line up even every inch or two so you can measure the width of the piece to be sure it is staying the same.
3. When a single color travels over a large area, use the lazy line technique. You also might need to use it when weaving the hems of large tapestries.
4. Bubble the weft more in larger areas than in smaller areas.

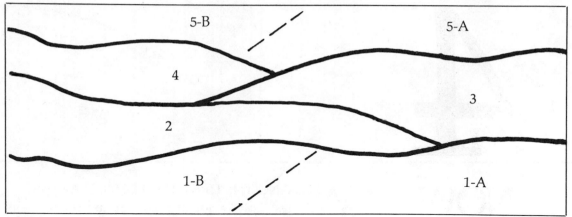

55A.

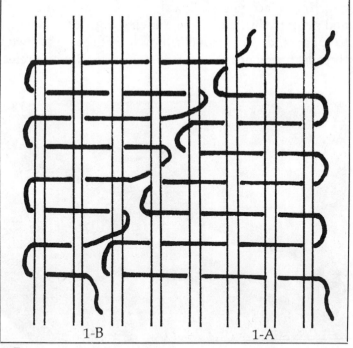

55B.

55. *Large design areas should be split into smaller areas. When woven this way, the edges of the tapestry will not draw in (A). Using this lazy line technique, the wefts are traveling in the same direction in the shed. First, area 1-A is woven for a few rows, then area 1-B is woven (B).*

4

NOW THE FUN BEGINS

WEAVING THE FIRST TWO DESIGN AREAS
At last, after a lot of planning and preparation, it's time to get started with the fun—the weaving of the tapestry.

First, place your full-scale cartoon under the warp and pin it to the hem of the weaving (fig. 56). Take care to push the pins straight down *between* the warp threads, trying not to penetrate the warp. (If you prefer,

56. The cartoon is placed behind the warp and pinned or sewn to the hem.

56.

you can sew the cartoon to the weaving with sewing thread, using large stitches.) Be sure the cartoon is even. The line you drew at the bottom of the cartoon will help you position it correctly. Even though you warped the loom at a width of thirteen inches, you may notice that the actual width is somewhat narrower. This usually happens and is nothing to be concerned about. However, the amount that the width draws in initially as weaving begins will become smaller and smaller as you gain more experience. If your warp is a little narrower, be sure to center the cartoon behind it. Before beginning, please read the remaining instructions and review the illustrations until you are asked to stop.

You will be weaving design area A first, at the left side of the cartoon. Remember, for this project you will weave from right to left in shed one and from left to right in shed two. It is not always necessary to weave in this manner, as you will see in the "Additional Tapestry Techniques" section in the next chapter. However, by following this procedure in the beginning, it will be easier for you to keep track of where you are.

Starting with a butterfly of color A, the weaving sequence is:

1. Open the shed (number one) and insert the

weft at the point where design area A begins, passing the weft from right to left (fig. 57A). Remember to leave a short end extending at the beginning of the area. Bubble the weft consistently and pack it in place.

2. Change the shed and pass the weft to the right edge of this design area, bubbling it consistently (don't forget to tuck in the end at the right edge), and pack the weft in place (fig. 57B).

Take care when setting the weft in place around the edge warp. It is easy for these first four or five warp threads to start pulling together. Be sure you are bubbling the weft consistently.

As you pass the weft through the shed, do not accidentally go over any of the warp threads that are in the *up* position, or under any of the warp threads that are in the *down* position. Use your hand to help open the shed wide enough so the weft can pass through easily.

Tip: When weaving with the weft traveling in the *same* direction and a design area is decreasing more than one warp at a time, all the warp ends will be covered if you have the first warp in the down position as the weft returns over its own design area. If you do not follow this procedure, one warp will be left exposed (not covered by the weft) where the two design areas meet (fig. 58A).

Do not forget the area between design areas. Set the weft around the edge warp of each individual design area just as carefully as you do around the edge warp. Just reach between the first and second warp of that area and press the weft to the weaving line. Watch the space between design areas to be sure that the warp threads do not start to pull apart. If they do, you are pulling the weft too tight.

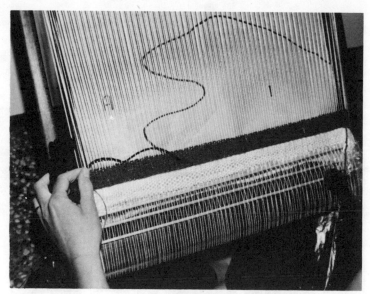

57A.

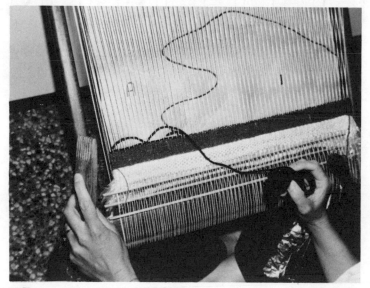

57B.

57. *Design area A is woven first because it is the decreasing area. Leaving a short end extending at the right, the weft is passed from right to left (A). As row two is woven, the end left extending on row one is woven back in over several warp threads (B).*

58. *When wefts are traveling in the same direction in the shed and the decreasing area is decreasing more than one warp at a time, the first warp of the decreasing area must be in the down position as the weft returns over its own design area. The sequence in A is incorrect and would cause an exposed warp to appear on row three at the point marked with an X. A solution to the problem is shown in B. By moving over one warp at a time, the warp threads get in the proper position to eliminate the exposed warp. Then as the design area moves over two warp threads, that first warp is in the down position.*

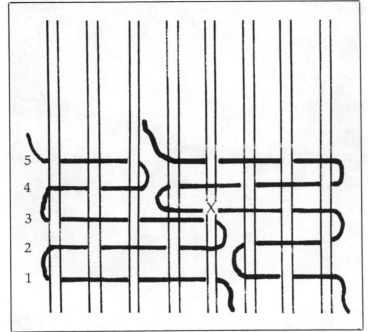

58A.

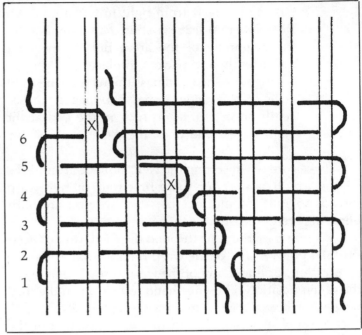

58B.

Stop now and weave this first part (approximately one inch) of design area A, following the outline of the cartoon as closely as possible (fig. 59).

Next, weave the adjoining area, design area one. As the size of area A decreases, this area will increase. When you finished weaving the hem, you left the butterfly of color one at the right edge of the tapestry. Remember, any time the weft is at the right edge of a particular design area, you know you should be weaving in shed one (weaving from right to left); if the weft is at the left of its design area, you start in shed two (weaving from left to right).

As you weave this adjoining area, do not increase its size a row too soon or an elongated stitch will appear where the two areas join. If the two adjoining areas are the same height before you advance one area over the other, this will not happen. At this point, there are two weft threads in the same shed. This always happens when weaving with the wefts traveling in the same direction in the same shed as one design area advances over its neighbor. This will not show as the weft is very tightly packed together.

Stop now and weave this area, bringing the weaving line up even across the entire width of the tapestry (fig. 60). Then measure the width of the piece to see if it is still the same width as it was when you finished the hem. Remember, if the piece is getting wider, you are bubbling the weft too much. If it is getting narrower, you are not bubbling the weft enough. Consistency is the key to success.

After you weave a little ways, it is a good idea to move the pins up, keeping the cartoon pinned as close to the weaving line as possible. This makes it easier to follow the lines on the cartoon and keeps the woven design from being distorted.

As you advance the warp around your loom or roll the warp forward, do not roll the cartoon along with the tapestry. Fold it back under itself to keep it out of the way.

YOU'RE ON YOUR OWN NOW

The steps you followed for weaving the first part of these first two design areas are the same steps you will follow as you continue to weave the tapestry. Follow the same sequence—regardless of how many design areas are across the row—weaving a design area at a time. Follow the outline of the design closely, changing colors where indicated.

The list of reminders below will act as a review of some key points and will help you weave a technically successful piece—one that has a flat, smooth surface (no ridges or bumps); straight, even edges; and a consistent texture throughout.

1. Bubble consistently on each row. This prevents ridges from appearing on the surface of the piece. Remember, the less elasticity the weft has, the larger the bubbles need to be.
2. Bubble larger design areas more than smaller areas.
3. The more design areas there are across a row, the less you bubble each individual area.
4. Pack the weft in the direction it travels.
5. Continue to check the tension of the warp. It will need to be tightened occasionally.

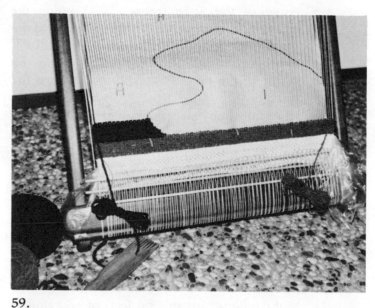

59.

60.

59. Area A is woven to the point where its direction changes.

60. Area one is woven next to area A. The width of the tapestry is measured each time the weaving line is brought up even.

6. Advance the warp frequently, keeping the weaving area directly in front of you. Feel the tension of the warp before and after you advance it to be sure it is the same. Measure the width of the tapestry after you advance the warp.

7. Use a lazy line in large design areas, especially those that travel the entire width of the tapestry (see "The Weaving Sequence" section in the preceding chapter).

8. Set the weft in place around the edge warp as well as between design areas.

9. Do not build up one area too high before weaving the adjoining area.

10. Measure the width of the piece each time the weaving line is built up evenly across the piece.

11. Make a habit, for this project, of weaving in the same direction in the same shed.

12. As you join a new weft, tuck the end to the back and overlap one or two warps, or select one of the other methods presented in the "Joining a New Weft" section in the preceding chapter.

13. Keep the cartoon pinned close to the weaving line.

14. Weave the decreasing design area first. (As you continue, you will begin weaving in design area one.)

15. Concentrate on being consistent with each and every process. Soon it will become automatic and require little thought.

The time has come to stop reading and weave the rest of the tapestry—you're on your own now. Have fun and I'll meet you "At the Top."

AT THE TOP

I know you now have spent quite a few hours weaving and that you are eager to see the finished tapestry off the loom. Only a few more things and you will be ready to do just that. Please continue reading until you are asked to stop.

Weave an additional inch past the top of the cartoon using color three. You will turn under this top hem when you finish the tapestry. After you weave the hem, secure the warp ends just as you did in the beginning. (See the "Securing Warp Ends" section in the preceding chapter if you need to review the technique for tying double half-hitches.)

Stop now and weave the hem and secure the warp ends.

Your tapestry is now ready to be removed from the loom. However, if you still have some unused warp on your loom and you want to try some of the other techniques presented in the next chapter, do not remove the tapestry from the loom. Just weave in a few more rows of plastic after you have tied the double half-hitches (to allow a couple of inches between your tapestry and your practice of other techniques). Then skip ahead to the "A Quick Review . . ." chapter. After you finish practicing the additional techniques, turn back to the "Cutting Off" section and follow the instructions for cutting off, finishing, and mounting your tapestry.

If you can't wait to see your finished tapestry off the loom, proceed to the next section, "Cutting Off," now.

CUTTING OFF

Removing the tapestry from the loom is an exciting experience, usually filled with both apprehension and anticipation. Regardless of the number of hours that have gone into the design and weaving of your tapestry, a part of you is woven into it, and sharing this moment with family and friends builds the excitement even more. When I studied at the San Francisco Tapestry Workshop one summer, everyone gathered around at the cutting off, sharing in the unveiling of the finished tapestry, seeing it in its entirety for the first time. Many times, an intricate and beautiful tapestry, woven in the traditional French Aubusson technique, would have taken several weavers two or three months to complete. Finishing such a piece called for a real celebration.

To remove your project from the loom, first remove the cartoon, then cut the warp threads about one inch above the row of double half-hitches you have just tied. Finish removing the piece by cutting the warp threads at the lower edge, just below the heading. After removing the heading material (which you can use again and again in other projects), trim these lower warp threads to a length of about one inch (fig. 61).

THE FINISHING TOUCHES

Lay the tapestry on a flat surface and let it rest for awhile. I usually leave a piece for twenty-four hours before finishing it. This allows it to relax after having been under constant tension while on the loom. When you measure the width, you will notice that it is slightly narrower than it was when it was on the loom. In addition, the length is also slightly shorter.

Steaming and Blocking

The next step is to steam the piece. I always steam my tapestries, even if they need no blocking, because I like the way it makes them feel and the nice finished look it gives them. You may want to use a damp cloth, although a steam iron will work as long as the piece is not extremely heavy. If you have an uneven edge, you

can block it at this time. If the edge goes in a little, steam that area and then stretch it a bit and let it dry. You can also "shrink" an area that is too wide when you use wool for the weft. If you use acrylic or other synthetic

61.

61. *When the tapestry has been removed from the loom, the warp ends are trimmed to about one inch. Double half-hitches will prevent the weft from unweaving.*

62. *To finish the bottom hem, the warp ends are tucked under the folded hem as it is hand stitched in place.*

63. *The top hem is folded down over the mounting board, the warp ends are tucked under, and the hem is stapled in place.*

materials, what you weave is what you get because you cannot steam or block most of these materials. After you have finished blocking your tapestry, let it dry completely before you move it.

Hemming, Mounting, and Hanging

When the tapestry is dry, fold under the bottom hem and tuck under the warp ends (fig. 62). Using a piece of weft color one and a large-eyed tapestry needle, hand stitch the hem in place, being careful not to allow the stitches to go through to the right side. The stitches do not need to be small and the yarn should be pulled snug, not tight.

Next, cut your mounting board so it is one-quarter inch narrower than the finished width of your tapestry, and sand it until it is smooth. Place the tapestry right side down on a flat, hard surface. Place the board one inch from the top, fold the hem down over the board, tuck the warp ends under, and staple or tack the tapestry to the mounting board (fig. 63).

If the weft ends extending out the back of the tapestry are long, you might want to trim them. Do not cut them too close—about an inch will do. As I weave, I always try to leave just a short end extending. This

62.

63.

saves a lot of time when weaving a large piece, because it eliminates the trimming of all those ends. Whenever possible, I weave in my ends (Navajo style), making the back look as good as the front.

The methods of securing warp ends, finishing, and mounting presented in this sample are only some of the ways of finishing tapestries. See the "Finishing, Mounting, and Tapestry Care" chapter to learn about other methods.

To hang the mounted tapestry, fold the mounting board down one turn so that the staples are away from you, facing the wall. Lift up the tapestry and nail the board directly to the wall (fig. 64). This makes a nice permanent mounting, with the tapestry hanging away from the wall just slightly.

Congratulations! I know your tapestry looks terrific. Although this is the end of this project, it is really just the beginning of your tapestry weaving. Now that you have the basics out of the way, I know you will want to try all the additional techniques that are described in the next chapter, which also can be used as an easy reference as you start your next few tapestries. So, on you go to "A Quick Review—And A Lot More."

64.

64. *For a nice permanent mounting, the mounting board is tacked to the wall.*

5

A QUICK REVIEW— AND A LOT MORE

A QUICK REVIEW

As you start working with an idea for your next tapestry, consider the total piece before you start weaving. What will be the design? (You can find tips on designing a tapestry in the "Creating a Design" chapter.) What size will it be? Which direction will you weave it—from the bottom to the top or sideways? Remember, it is easier to weave horizontal design lines than vertical ones. Will you weave it with the right side facing you? Will it have fringe? How heavy will it be? How will you finish and mount it? If it is a large piece, will your method of mounting support it correctly?

When figuring the width of the warp, allow a little extra to compensate for the amount the edges will draw in as weaving begins. This will vary depending on the materials and the type of loom you use. Remember, too, that the width of the finished piece will be slightly narrower when it is removed from the loom.

The length of the tapestry will also draw up slightly when it is removed from the loom and be a little shorter than the cartoon. Depending on what materials you use and how tight you pack the weft, this will vary from approximately one-half to one inch for every thirty inches in length.

Using wefts of a similar size and elasticity makes it easier to control the edge and surface of the piece, making the tapestry more consistent than if you were to use a variety of wefts. As you experiment with other weft materials, you will learn how much bubbling is necessary for each kind.

The basic sequence involved in weaving a tapestry is:

1. Design and prepare a cartoon.
2. Calculate warp and estimate weft quantities.
3. Select the materials. If you are not sure how some colors will work together, weave a few color samples.
4. Tightly and evenly warp the loom. You might want to use a double warp at each edge.
5. Weave a heading to space the warp threads evenly.
6. Secure the warp ends.
7. Weave the hem.
8. Add fringe, if desired.
9. Weave, and measure frequently.
10. Weave a hem at the top and secure the warp ends.
11. Remove the tapestry (remembering not to cut the warp ends too close) and let it rest for a

65.

65. *Tapestries are used in many public places today. Each of the five tapestries in this series is five by three and one-half feet. All were woven in a sideways direction and include many of the additional techniques (as shown later in detail photos of these tapestries) that are presented in this chapter. (Woven by the author)*

while.

12. Add the finishing touches—steaming (and blocking, if necessary), hemming, and mounting.
13. Hang the finished piece in that special place.
14. Get started on the next inspiration.

A SUMMARY OF THE TIPS

To achieve technical excellence quickly and easily, remember the following:

1. Be sure the warp is tight and under consistent tension as this helps eliminate many problems. It makes it easier to control the edge and surface of the tapestry than if the warp were loose or uneven, helps keep the warp threads evenly spaced, and allows the weft to pack down evenly.
2. Use a double warp at each selvedge, if desired, as double warps add strength and evenness to the tapestry.
3. The larger the weft, the wider you space the warp; the finer the weft, the closer you space the warp.
4. When using wefts with different amounts of elasticity, bubble the weft with little elasticity more than the weft with a lot of elasticity.
5. Bubble the weft a little more in larger design areas than in smaller areas.
6. Bubble the weft consistently on each row. This prevents ridges from forming on the surface of the tapestry.
7. Press the point of each bubble close to the previous weaving line but do not allow a loop of weft to appear on the surface.
8. Pack the weft in the direction it travels. This helps control the amount of weft needed on each row and eliminates the possibility of loops extending at the edge of the piece or at the edge of each individual design area.
9. Hold the weft in place as it wraps around the edge warp as well as when it wraps around the edge warp of each design area.
10. Make small butterflies as they tangle less and pass through the shed more easily than large butterflies.
11. Use a finer weft for the hem and weave a hem of at least one inch to give a flat finish to the hemmed edge.
12. Always start weaving the decreasing shape or design area first and continue weaving in a design area until the direction of the design changes.
13. If a design area is several inches high, weave an inch or so and then weave the adjoining area, bringing the weaving line up even.
14. Be sure the height of adjoining areas is even before advancing one over the other.
15. Use lazy lines when working with large design areas, especially when the weft travels the entire width of the piece. This keeps the edges from pulling in. On larger pieces, it is a good idea to use this technique when weaving the hem.
16. Keep the cartoon pinned close to the weaving line as this helps eliminate distortion of the design.
17. Advance the warp frequently, keeping the weaving area directly in front of you.
18. Measure the width of the piece often as edge control is difficult in your first few projects.
19. Plan ahead.

ADDITIONAL TAPESTRY TECHNIQUES

The tapestry in the sample project was quite simple in design, allowing you to concentrate on the technical aspects of weaving and yarn control. Any tapestry, regardless of how intricate it is, can be woven in this same manner, building up a design area at a time. There are also, however, many other tapestry techniques, which can be used by themselves or in combination with one another. Some are more challenging to weave than others, but each one adds something special to your tapestries.

Some of these techniques require that you weave two or more areas concurrently. Some are woven with the wefts traveling in the same direction in the shed while others are worked with the wefts traveling in opposite directions in the same shed; some can be woven both ways.

I have included a description and illustration of each technique (both ways when applicable). As you try these various methods, weave them both ways in order to understand the effect that each process creates. When I weave a tapestry, I select the technique and method of weaving that best fit each situation. I do not always weave with the weft traveling in the same or opposite directions. In fact, I often use both procedures in the same tapestry. I encourage you to try each technique, both ways, to find out which you like best. Remember, you are limited only by your imagination. If you try it and it works for you, then do it.

Many of these techniques are known by different names and you will notice in some cases that I have listed more than one name for a technique. I am sure, as your study of tapestry continues, you will discover other names for each of these techniques. You might even make up a few of your own.

To help you eliminate potential problems, I have provided technical tips throughout this chapter, as in the other chapters. Since tapestries can be woven from the front (with the right side facing you as you weave) or from the back (with the wrong side facing you), the tips regarding warp position will vary depending on the way you choose to weave. Unless otherwise indicated, the tips given always apply to weaving with the front

66.

66. *Measuring thirty-four by twenty-three inches, this tapestry was woven in the slit technique on a nail-frame loom. The warp is cotton seine twine set at six ends per inch and the weft is handspun wool. (Woven by Shirley Rutherford of Sacramento, California)*

side facing you. If you are weaving with the back side facing you, these tips should be reversed. For example, if the instructions say "the first warp in the up position" and you are weaving from the back, the first warp would be in the down position.

As you experiment with various weaving and shading techniques, be sure to keep notes about your discoveries so you do not have to "reinvent" them later on.

Slit

When using the building-up technique of weaving, a barely visible slit is created where two design areas meet. When two areas are woven in this manner for more than several rows, a vertical slit occurs between the two areas. The wefts are woven back and forth within their respective design areas. Since the two areas are woven independently of one another, one can be

woven for several inches and then the other can be woven, or the two areas can be woven row by row within their own area. The wefts can travel in the same or opposite directions in the same shed (fig. 67).

In figure 68, in which the wefts are traveling in the same direction, you will notice that when design area B passes over design area A, there are two wefts in the same shed on that row. This always happens when working the wefts in the same direction. It is not an error (most Navajo weaving is worked with the wefts traveling in the same direction) and will not cause a problem unless the weft you are working with is too heavy and cannot be packed tight enough to cover the warp. However, if you prefer not to have these two wefts in the same shed, you can break weft A on row four after it wraps around warp six and weave the end in or tuck it to the back, eliminating the double weft in the

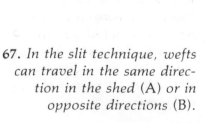

67. *In the slit technique, wefts can travel in the same direction in the shed* (A) *or in opposite directions* (B).

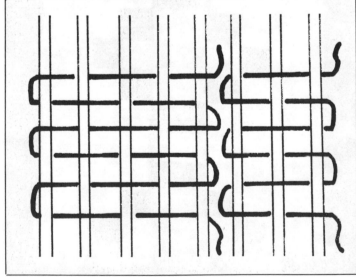

67A.

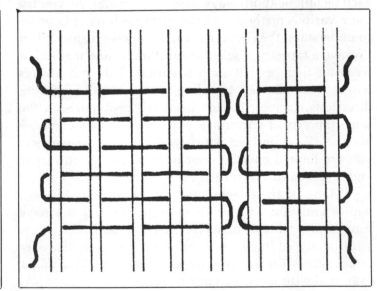

67B.

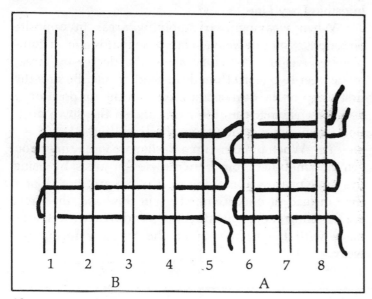

1 2 3 4 5 6 7 8
   B   A

68.
shed.

When wefts are worked in opposite directions in the shed (fig. 69), B is already in the opposite shed when it passes over A. Remember, when weaving in this manner, work each adjoining area in the opposite direction from its neighbor (fig. 70). Open the shed and start area A with the weft traveling to the right, while weft B travels to the left, weft C to the right, weft D to the left, and weft E to the right, all in the same shed opening.

Tip: When using wefts of the same size, each area meets the adjoining area, pass for pass. If wefts are not of equal size, it might take two or more passes of a fine weft to equal one pass of a heavier weft.

When weaving these slits, be sure that the warp does not start to separate where this slit is created. A good tight warp (the tighter the better) and consistent bubbling make it easy to weave perfect slits.

If you are weaving the tapestry sideways, you will need to sew the slits together from the back side when the tapestry is finished because the slits will be horizontal when the piece is hung. If they are not sewn, the piece will have many weak areas, and the slits will separate, causing the tapestry to sag. If, however, you are weaving the tapestry from the bottom to the top and the piece will remain vertical when it is hung, it is not necessary to sew the slits together. (All the vertical lines in the piece shown in figure 71 were woven using the slit tapestry technique and were not sewn together.)

If you feel that the slits will weaken the piece, regardless of which way it is woven, sew them together (see the "Finishing" section in the "Finishing, Mounting, and Tapestry Care" chapter) or weave these areas using the weft interlock or warp interlock techniques, which are described in this chapter.

68. *Two wefts are in the same shed when wefts are traveling in the same direction as one area passes over the other.*

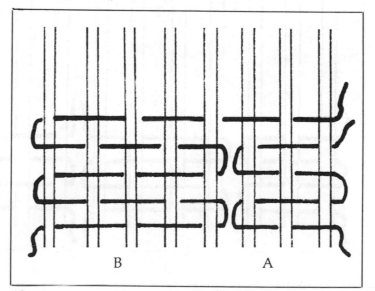

B   A

69.

69. *Only one weft is in the shed when wefts are traveling in opposite directions and one area passes over the other.*

Reversing Weft Direction

When weaving with the wefts traveling in opposite directions in the shed, a problem can arise when a new design area must be woven in between two existing areas, as in figure 72. As the design is started, you weave areas A and B in opposite directions. As area C begins, you must reverse the direction of either A or B in order to continue weaving all neighboring areas in opposite directions. To correct the situation, loop the weft (on the wrong side of the tapestry) across its design area and pass it through the shed in the opposite direction (fig. 73). For example, you should weave row four of design area B from right to left, but introducing area C makes it necessary to reverse the direction of this area. Loop it across the back and weave it in a left to right direction.

Invisible Lazy Line

When weaving two adjoining areas in opposite directions, you can weave a lazy line that is almost completely invisible. As you weave the decreasing area, move over two warp threads instead of one. Be sure the first warp of the decreasing area is in the up position if you are weaving from the front and in the down position if you are weaving from the back (fig. 74).

Tip: When building up a design area at a time, you get the smoothest join between design areas by using this same process of moving over two warp threads at a time instead of one. Remember, in this case, the wefts are traveling in opposite directions and weaving is taking place with the right side of the tapestry facing the weaver.

70. *When weaving with wefts traveling in opposite directions in the shed, each area is worked in the opposite direction of its neighbor.*

71. *Woven on a floor loom, this slit tapestry has a cotton 3/2 warp set at six ends per inch and a wool weft. It is twenty-nine by thirty-nine inches.*

72. *When wefts are traveling in opposite directions and a new design area is introduced, the direction of the weft in one of the adjoining areas must be reversed.*

73. *To reverse the direction of the weft, loop the weft (on the back side of the tapestry) across its design area and pass it through the shed in the opposite direction.*

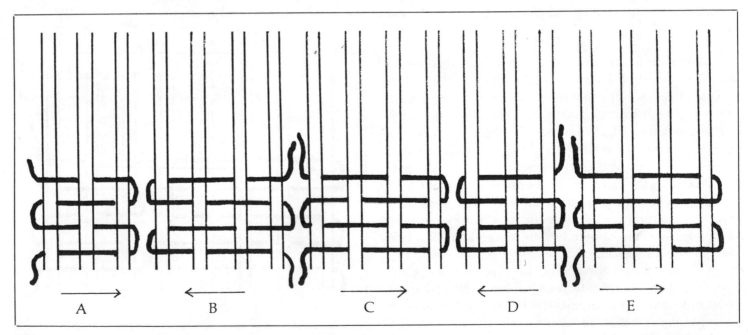

A → B ← C → D ← E →

70.

Weft Interlock (Hooked Joint or Vertical Lock)

When two design areas meet for a long vertical distance and you do not want the slit to occur between design areas, use this technique. The wefts interlock around each other between warp threads, causing a little serrated edge at the point of interlock (fig. 75).

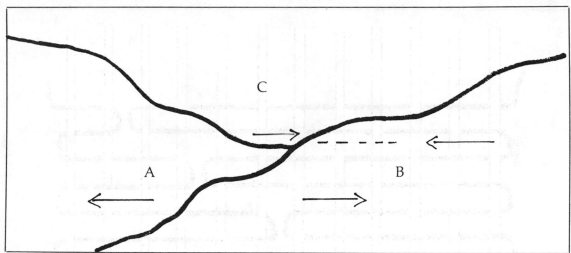

72.

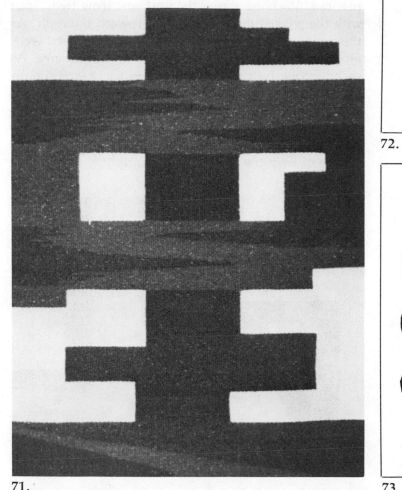

71.

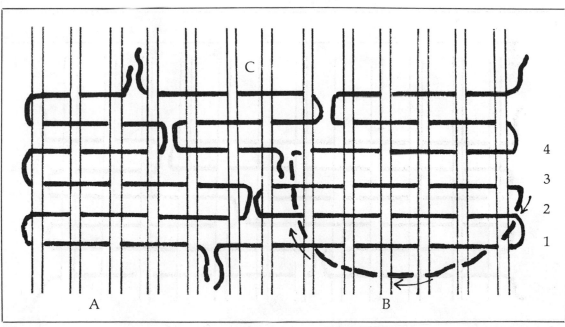

73.

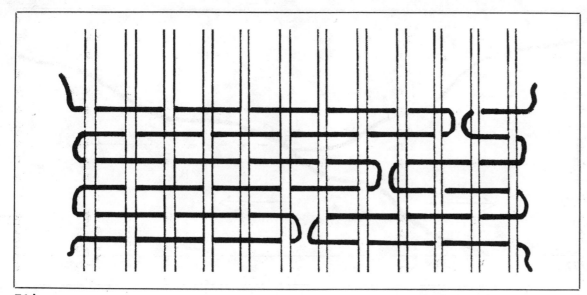

74A.

This technique can be worked with the weft traveling in the same or opposite directions. I find it easier to learn when the wefts are traveling in the same direction, especially if more than two areas are involved, as in figure 76A. In this illustration, you work five separate design areas across the row in the same direction. The weft for each design area is at the left edge at the end of row one. Weaving across the next row (row two), start with the weft at the left, weaving toward the right. As this weft reaches its neighbor, lay it over the next weft, pick up this weft, and weave it toward the next area. As each weft meets its neighbor, an interlock of wefts occurs (fig. 76B). To start the next row (row three), begin again with the leftmost weft and work each design area toward the left. Notice that *the interlock occurs every other row* (rows two, four, and so on in this example). It is easy to keep track of when the interlock should take

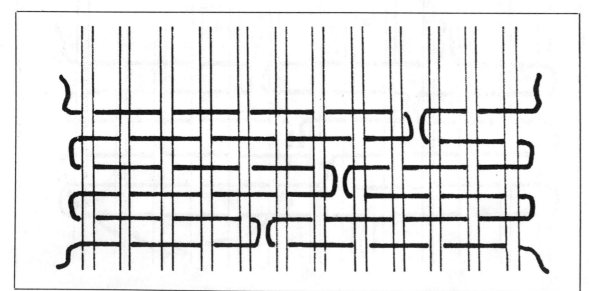

74B.

75.

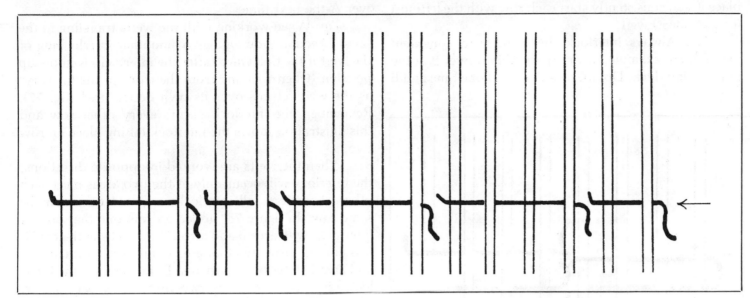

76A.

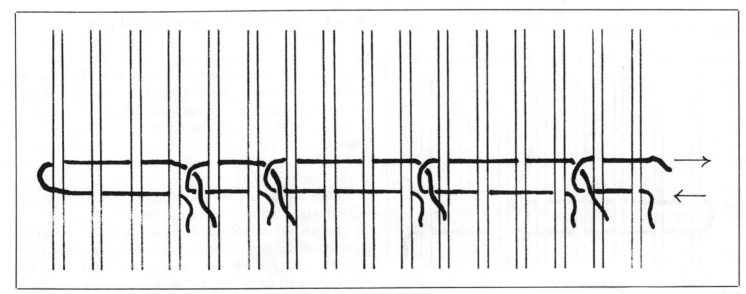

76B.

74. *A less visible lazy line can be achieved when weaving two adjoining areas in opposite directions by moving over two warps each row instead of one. The first warp of the decreasing area should be in the up position as the weft returns over its own design area when weaving from the front of the tapestry (A) and in the down position when weaving from the back of the tapestry (B).*

75. *This tapestry detail illustrates the weft interlock technique. Note the serrated edge where design areas meet.*

76. *In using the weft interlock technique, no interlock takes place on row one and the wefts are worked from right to left in each area (A). As the areas meet in row two, the wefts interlock (B).*

place if you consistently start each row with the leftmost (or rightmost) weft.

Tip: Always interlock the wefts in a consistent manner. For example, always pass weft A over B at the point of interlock. Do not pass A over B one time and B over A the next time.

Tip: When working with the wefts traveling in the same direction, you will get a smoother interlocking of the weft if the first warp (after the interlock) is in the up position (when weaving from the front of the tapestry) as the weft returns over its own design area (fig. 77). Remember, the interlock occurs every other row and this illustration shows the interlock taking place on row two.

When the wefts are worked in opposite directions, the interlock will occur only as the two areas meet each other. Therefore, all interlocks will not occur on the same row. In figure 78, notice on row one that area A interlocks with area B and area C interlocks with area D. It is not until row two that area B interlocks with area C and area D interlocks with area E. Remember, the interlock takes place only as two areas meet each other. There is no interlock as they go away from each other.

Warp Interlock (Dovetailing or Turned Joint)

With this technique, the wefts in adjoining areas turn around a common warp thread. This causes a larger serrated edge (where two areas join) than the interlocking weft technique, but it is a good method to use when weaving diagonal lines (see the next section); because no slit occurs between areas, the join is stronger. This technique is not recommended, however, for long vertical joins, because an area of buildup occurs as the common warp is wrapped by both wefts. This technique can be woven with the weft traveling in the same direction or opposite directions.

To weave several adjoining areas, with the wefts traveling in the same direction using this technique, start weaving with the leftmost weft on one row and the rightmost weft on the next row. For example, in figure

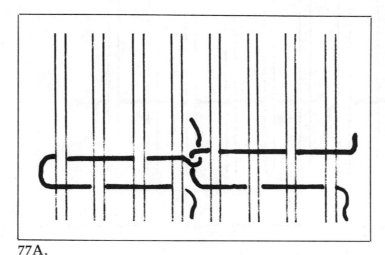

77A.

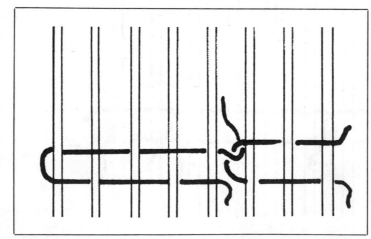

77B.

77. When weaving from the front of the tapestry and the wefts are traveling in the same direction, a smooth interlock occurs when the first warp after the interlock is in the up position. The interlock takes place on row two (A). When weaving from the back of the tapestry, a smooth interlock occurs when the first warp is in the down position (B).

79, weaving from right to left on row one, start with weft A, then weave weft B. On row two, weave weft B first (weaving toward the right), then weft A. Be sure the wefts in neighboring areas go around the same warp (warp five in this example). Start row three with weft A and row four with weft B, and so on.

When the wefts are traveling in opposite directions, make a complete pass of two rows with the weft (fig. 80) before weaving the adjoining area.

Tip: The excessive buildup created with this tech-

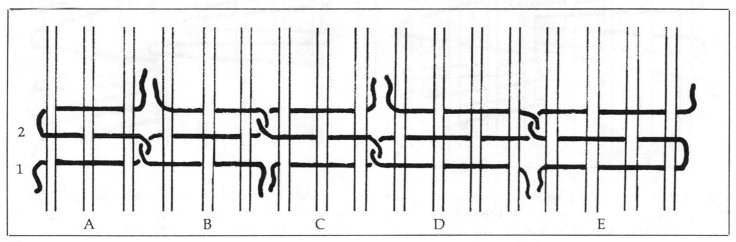

78.

78. *When wefts are traveling in opposite directions, the interlock occurs only as areas meet one another.*

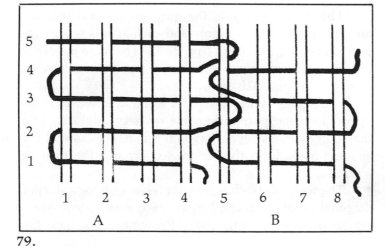

79.

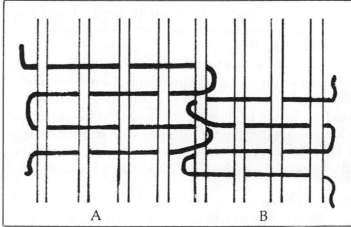

80.

79. *With wefts being worked in the same direction, the warp interlock is started by weaving with the leftmost weft on one row and the rightmost weft on the next row.*

80. *When using the warp interlock and the wefts are being worked in opposite directions, a complete pass of two rows is made with one weft before the adjoining area is woven.*

81. Buildup caused by the warp interlock can be lessened by weaving several rows of one area before weaving the adjoining area, but this increases the serrated appearance (A). Using the technique shown here (B) will lessen the serrated effect. Notice that the second pass is not woven as far as the first and third passes.

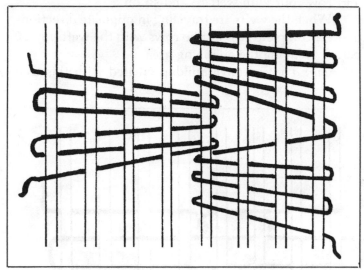

81A.

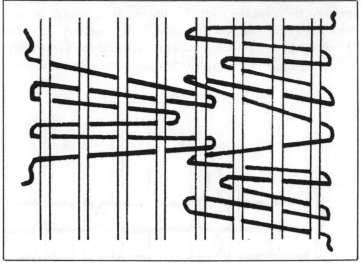

81B.

nique can be lessened by weaving two or three passes (four or six rows) with one weft before weaving the adjoining area (fig. 81). This increases the serrated edge, but that can be lessened somewhat by the alternate method shown in the illustration, in which the second pass is woven one warp less than the first and third passes. Therefore, fewer rows are woven around the common warp thread.

I find it faster and easier to weave with the wefts traveling in the same direction when I am using a loom with a rigid heddle or any loom that does not have foot treadles. In the beginning, it is easier to keep track of what you are doing when weaving with many discontinuous wefts across the entire width of the tapestry if they all are traveling in the same direction in the same shed.

Diagonal Lines

All of the techniques mentioned so far can be

woven diagonally as well as vertically. Many combinations are shown in figures 82 through 84. For the sake of simplicity, the wefts in figures 82 and 83 travel in opposite directions, but remember, they can be woven either way.

The slit technique is the quickest method because one area is built up at a time and each area is woven independently of the other (fig. 82A). To create a steeper diagonal, several rows can be woven before moving over a warp (fig. 82B).

A diagonal worked around a common warp (warp interlock) gives a smoother line on a gradual diagonal than it does on a steeper diagonal (fig. 83) because of the amount of buildup that is caused around the turning warp.

The weft interlock is a better technique for a steeper diagonal in which several rows are woven before moving over a warp (fig. 84). Remember, to get the

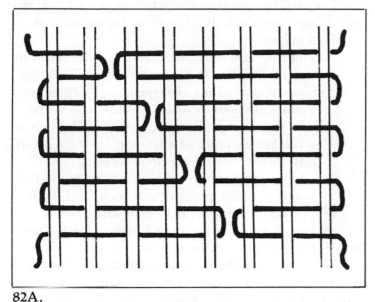

82A.

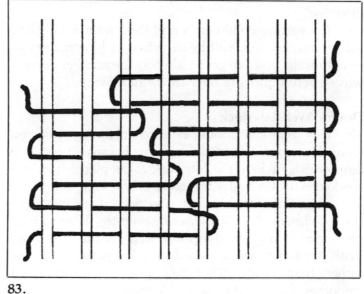

83.

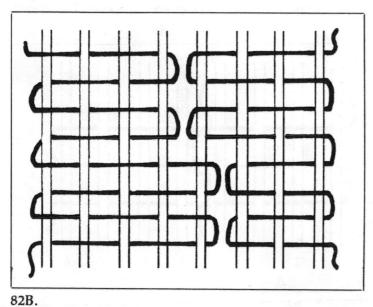

82B.

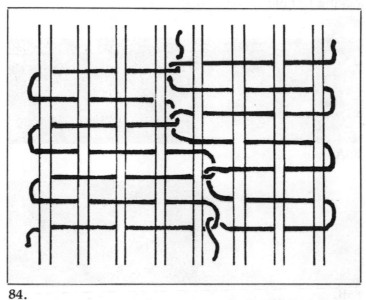

84.

82. *Using the slit technique, a gradual diagonal line occurs when moving over one warp with each pass (A). For a steeper diagonal, weave two (or more) passes before moving over a warp (B).*

83. *When using the warp interlock, a smoother line is created on a gradual diagonal than on a steep diagonal due to the buildup created by both wefts circling the same warp.*

84. *The weft interlock works well on a steep diagonal since less buildup occurs as the wefts interlock between warp threads.*

smoothest turn, always interlock the wefts in the same direction.

Try various combinations of these interlocking and slit techniques. You will be surprised at how many different results you can get by altering the number of rows woven before moving over to the next warp.

Double Weft Interlock

This technique should be used only when weaving from the wrong side of the tapestry because it causes a bumpy ridge where the interlock takes place. It is best worked with the wefts traveling in the same direction. When using the double weft interlock (as distinct from the weft interlock), start weaving with the leftmost weft on one row and the rightmost weft on the next row. With this technique, an interlock takes place *every* row rather than every other row and creates a much smoother join on the right side than any other interlocking technique (fig. 85).

The step-by-step process involved in weaving the double weft interlock is shown in figure 86 and is described below:

1. In row one, start with weft B, weaving from right to left. At the point of interlock (between warps four and five), place weft A over weft B as weft A weaves to the left.
2. In row two, start with weft A and when it reaches the point of interlock, lay it over weft B. Pick up B and continue weaving.
3. In row three, start with weft B, laying weft B over A at the point of interlock, and so on.

Try to form the interlock in a consistent manner—A over B on one row, then B over A on the next row, as the interlock occurs on every row.

This technique also can be worked with the wefts traveling in opposite directions. If you should find yourself in this situation, simply change the shed at the point of interlock. As you can see, however, it is easier

85. The double weft interlock is one technique that must be woven from the back side of the tapestry because a bumpy ridge forms where the interlock occurs (A). On the right side, however, the point of interlock is a smooth line (B), much smoother than any other interlocking technique.

86. In the double weft interlock technique, the interlock takes place every row.

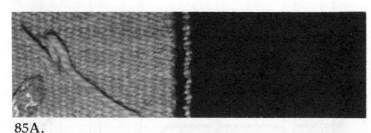
85A.

85B.

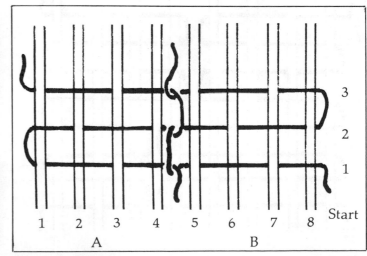
86.

and quicker to weave with the wefts traveling in the same direction.

Double Weft Interlock around a Single Warp

When designing a tapestry, try to avoid having narrow design lines that travel in the direction of the warp. These narrow warp-way lines are difficult to weave successfully. However, if you find you need to weave a narrow vertical line, you can use a variation of the double weft interlock. Remembering the process just described, look at figure 87. On row one, weft A passes under warp seven as the shed is opened. On row two, weave weft B first and when it reaches the point of interlock (between warps six and seven), pass it over weft A. At this point, do not weave weft A, because the interlock is taking place around a single warp. On row three, weft A starts the row, passing under warp seven. You then lay it over weft B, forming the interlock, and weave weft B to the left. When using this technique, the adjoining area (weft C in this case) is woven using the slit technique and sewn together when the tapestry is finished. Using three colors, area A becomes a vertical design area the width of a single warp. Remember, narrow vertical design lines are difficult to weave; try to avoid them when designing your tapestries.

Because they require that many adjacent areas be worked at the same time, these interlocking techniques are more time-consuming to weave than the slit technique. However, if you are using the beater on your loom to pack the weft in place or if you enjoy weaving a row at a time, you may prefer these interlocking techniques.

Outlining

To accent a design area or to break two design areas

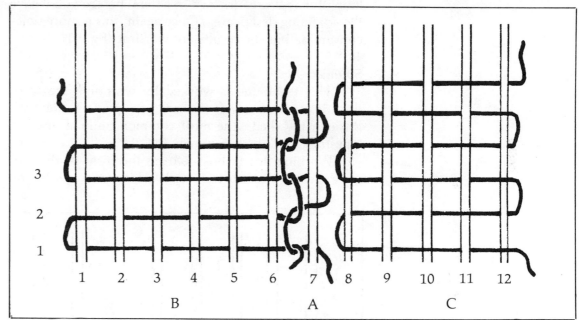

87.

of the same color, try outlining. Weave the area to be outlined first, then, with a contrasting color, weave two or more rows around the area to be outlined (fig. 88). Be sure to allow a little extra weft around these curved areas. If you weave one row of the outlining weft, you will get a broken line instead of a solid line. The detail photograph of the tapestry in figure 89 shows a variety of techniques: outlining with multiple rows over the mountains, outlining with single rows on the rooftops, and using the slit and weft interlock methods on the edges of the building.

Outlining is a good way to break up a solid area, making it more interesting. It requires that you break the design into separate and distinct parts (fig. 90). After you finish weaving each numbered area, weave the out-

87. *A double weft interlock around a single warp may be used to weave a very narrow vertical line.*

lining for that area (shown in letters) before you weave the adjoining design area. Once again, this is more time-consuming but the results are worth it (fig. 91).

Soumak

This technique is worked by wrapping the warp threads with the weft rather than passing the weft through the shed. The most common Soumak used in tapestry is the single Soumak.

Working this technique from the front of the tapestry creates a raised texture. Working one row in one direction and the next row in the opposite direction produces a twill effect. Weaving from the back of the piece results in a perfectly smooth horizontal line forming on the front of the tapestry where the two rows meet.

When working a single Soumak, as in figure 92, pass the weft from left to right, over and around under warp one, then over and around under warp two, and so on, across the row or design area. The weft actually passes over two warps and back under one. Row one shows the Soumak stitch being worked from left to right and row two shows it being done from right to left.

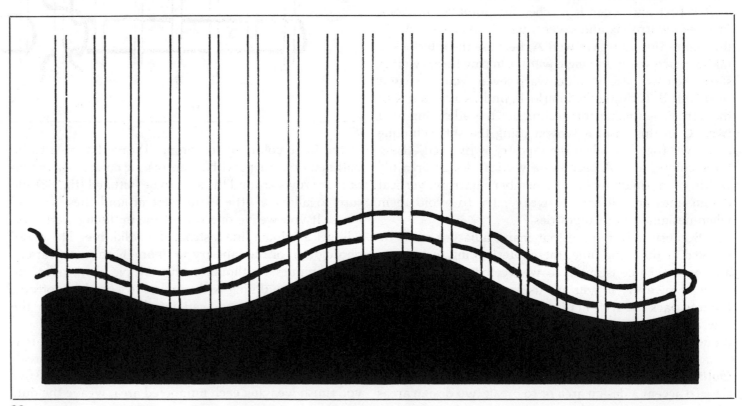

88. *With outlining, the area to be outlined is woven first, then a contrasting weft is woven for several rows in order to outline the shape.*

88.

You can vary the stitch by working it in different combinations. For example, you can go over and around under the same warp several times before moving to the next warp. You also can vary the number of warps over which the weft travels before it comes back under. For example, it can travel over four, then back around and under two.

Tip: If you are going to weave a border around all four edges of your tapestry, you might want to try this. Weaving with the back of the tapestry facing you as you work, use double weft interlock on the vertical border lines and two rows of Soumak on the horizontal border lines. Work one row of the horizontal border (with the border color) in one direction and the next row (in the background color) in the opposite direction. This will result in very smooth lines showing between the border and the background color on the front of the tapestry.

Horizontal Stripes

Small horizontal stripes can be achieved quite easily by weaving two rows of one color and then two rows of another color. When using this technique, be sure that all warp threads are covered at the edge. If you start these two colors in opposite directions, you can pass one color around the other at the edge (fig. 94).

Vertical Stripes (Pick and Pick)

To weave narrow vertical stripes, weave one row of one color and then one row of the other color. Weaving

89.

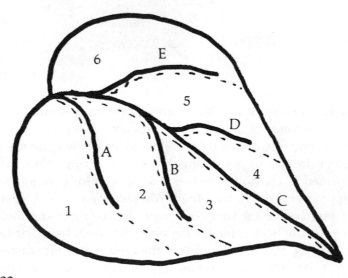

90.

89. *This tapestry detail highlights various techniques: slit and weft interlock on the edges of the building, and outlining over the mountains and on the rooftops. The tapestry has a cotton warp set at eight ends per inch and a wool weft.*

90. *Outlining shapes within a shape requires that each individual area be woven separately and then outlined. The small dotted lines indicate how the shape was divided into individual areas.*

91.

woven entirely in this technique. (The design in this rug is referred to as "coal mine raised edge.")

Shading Techniques—Hatching and Hachure

To shade areas and make a gradual transition from one color area to another, try hatching. The wefts are worked in opposite directions and each one makes a complete pass (two rows) before the adjoining area is woven. For example, in figure 97A, areas A and B are each woven for a complete pass in their own area, then area A passes over area B as far as desired. Next, area B is woven to meet area A and then another pass of B is woven over A. Then A is woven to meet B, followed by another pass of A, which is woven over area B, and so on. Hatching can be woven in a regular or irregular pattern (fig. 97), using a combination of passes and turning points to create an unlimited number of effects. Several combinations are shown in the detail photographs in figure 98.

The hachure technique is similar to hatching and is frequently seen in French tapestries. It takes several passes to weave a complete sequence and is worked with

91. This detail photo shows the benefits of using the outlining technique.

92. In the single Soumak technique, the weft passes over two warps and back under one.

only one row of a color creates a broken or dotted line when several of these dotted lines are woven in succession (one row of one color followed by a row of another color in the opposite shed). Vertical stripes thus are formed as the dotted lines of the same color continue to appear one above the other. You will get a smooth edge if you weave the first color from left to right and then weave the next color (in the opposite shed) from left to right (fig. 95). At the edge of the area, one weft crosses over the other. The Navajo rug shown in figure 96 was

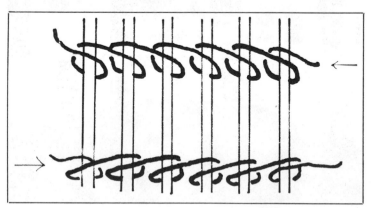

92.

93.

93. *"The Rockies, Alberta" was done entirely in the Soumak technique. It was woven on a seventy-one-inch Swedish floor loom using a wool-mohair warp set at seven ends per inch and a wool weft. It is four by seven and one-half feet. (Woven by Ellie Fidler of Berkeley, California. Photo by Paul Buer)*

the wefts traveling in opposite directions, as in figure 99. Weave weft one for three complete passes, stopping at point A. Then weave weft two for a total of five passes, stopping at point B. Continue with weft one from point A to point C, and so on. This example has created a three-pointed regular hachure, indicated by the turning points marked with an X. This technique can be woven in either regular or irregular patterns (fig. 100) and can have a different number of turning points.

You will have a lot of fun combining these tech-niques. For a real challenge, try weaving several groups of hachures at the same time.

Combining Weft Yarns for Shading

Still other shading effects can be created by using several strands of weft as a single weft. These multiple wefts are wound together into butterflies or onto bobbins and woven as a single strand. Be sure the strands are wound evenly and consistently. If they are not, bumps of weft will appear on the surface of the tapestry.

The random twisting of the weft that occurs during weaving makes one color dominant in one place and a different color dominant in another place. Even more subtle shading can be created by combining this multiple strand technique with hatching. (An example of this is

94. *In using the horizontal stripes technique, care must be taken to make sure all warp threads are covered at the edge. Weave two rows of each color, starting them at opposite edges. Bold and fine lines have been used to illustrate two different weft colors.*

95. *In weaving small vertical stripes, the first color is woven from left to right and the next color is woven from left to right in the opposite shed. Bold and fine lines have been used to illustrate two different weft colors.*

96. *This Navajo rug was woven using the "coal mine raised edge" or vertical stripes technique. The warp is wool and the weft is wool spun from natural-colored fleece. Natural dyes were used. (Weaver unknown. From the collection of the author)*

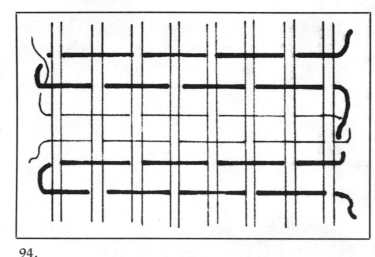

94.

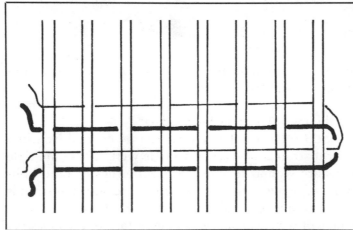

95.

96.

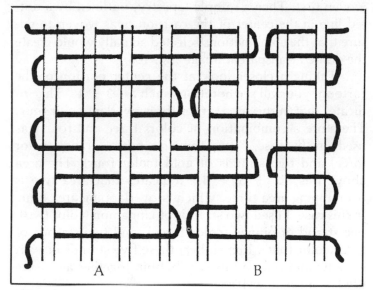

97A.

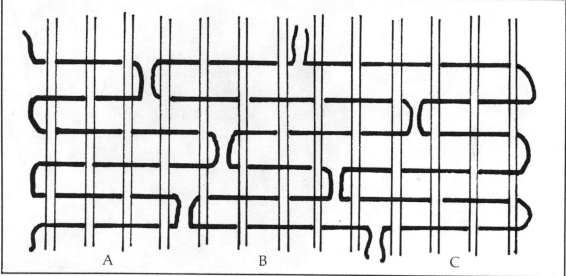

97C.

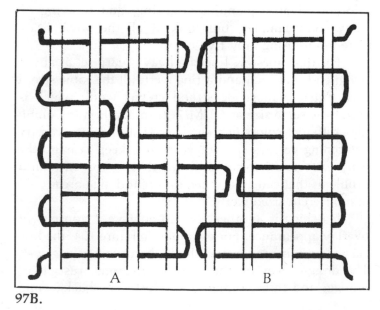

97B.

illustrated in the tapestry "White Petunias," plate 3A in the color section of this book.)

Transparent Shading

Shading techniques can be used to create a transparent appearance in part or all of a tapestry. Try varying the combination of colors as you work from one area to the next. The cartoon in figure 102 has many shapes overlapping each other. For the sake of clarity, I have drawn the shapes with different sized marking pens to make it easier for you to identify each shape. The only solid area, number five, is the background. The other shapes are numbered one, two, three, and four. The following were the colors used: one, brown; two, cinnamon; three, orange; four, gold; and five, cream.

Many color samples of various combinations of the five weft colors (using five strands of weft as one) were

97. Hatching can be woven in a regular pattern (A), in an irregular pattern (B), and in several areas at a time (C).

98A.

98B.

98. *Several combinations of hatching are shown in these detail photos. Because hatching takes place on the horizontal while weaving, both of these tapestries were woven sideways. Irregular hatching is illustrated in the petals of the poppy (A) while a randomly spaced regular hatching is shown in the leaves (B).*

woven first. Then a sample tapestry, outlined by a dotted line in the center of the cartoon, was woven to ensure that the combinations selected actually would create the desired transparent image (fig. 103).

Taking a closer look at the center portion of the cartoon, you will see notations such as "3 + 4." This indicates that in this area, color three overlaps color four. Therefore a combination of colors three and four was used. In this case, I used three strands of orange (color three) and two strands of gold (color four). The area above this, "2 + 3 + 4," indicates that area two is overlapping area three, which is overlapping area four. In this case, I used two strands of cinnamon (color two), one strand of orange (color three), and two strands of gold (color four). Remember, these five strands of weft were wound onto a tapestry bobbin together and were used as a single weft.

Yes, you are absolutely right. This project required a lot of advance planning, figuring, and weaving of many color samples, but look at all the possibilities there are in using only five colors.

For this tapestry, I used a heavy warp set at about seven ends per inch and a fine weft, all the same size. I used Paternayan single strand crewel wool, which is about the same size as CUM 7/2. In addition to combining different colors in a single weft strand, you can try combining various sizes of yarn. Just keep in mind the warp-weft relationship and watch out for structural problems that can arise when different design areas contain different sized wefts.

Hatching is another way to achieve a transparent overlay appearance. For example, in figure 104, the low curved area is orange and the high curved area is rust. The design areas on the cartoon are: one, rust; two, orange; and three, orange over rust. The background color four is white. The weaving sequence, working with the wefts traveling in opposite directions, is:

1. Weave a pass (two rows) of weft color two through areas two and three. Then weave a pass of color two across only its own design area.
2. With color one, weave a pass in only its design area and then weave a pass that travels through design areas one and three.
3. Repeat these two steps throughout the overlay portion.

If you select colors of too great a contrast when using this technique, the transparent area will appear as horizontal stripes. This can be eliminated if the yarn has a little texture, is tweed, or is irregular in size. Handspun works very well, especially if it is unevenly spun and

99. Hachures are another form of hatching. Regular hachures form a consistent pattern.

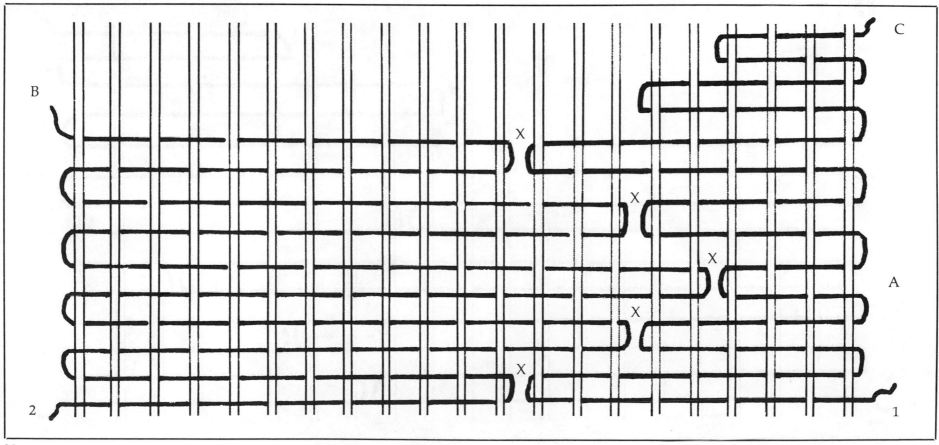

99.

unblocked, because it visually breaks up the horizontal image that might appear. When using colors with a more subtle contrast, the horizontal stripes, created by weaving two rows of one color and two rows of another, are not noticeable.

100. *Hachures may form an irregular pattern also.*

SOME FUN WITH HANDSPUN

Taking detailed notes to keep track of your experiments with different techniques and fibers is always important. This is also true when working with handspun. These yarns will change the image and overall appearance of your previous discoveries even when you use the same weaving techniques. As you gain experience and confidence, try using handspun of different textures in the same tapestry.

Spinning and dyeing your own yarn is rewarding,

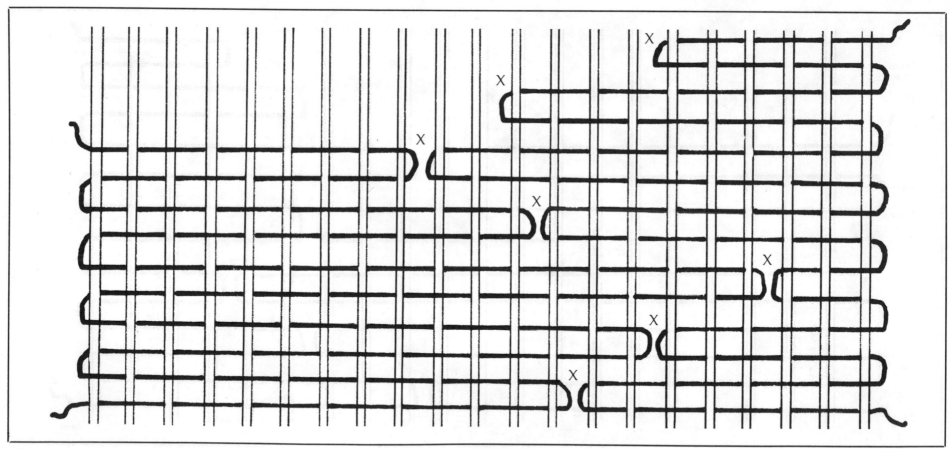

100.

101.

but creating a tapestry with handspun weft that you have created yourself is even more gratifying. It also makes us appreciate our ancestors, many of whom spun all their own yarn for knitting and weaving. If you spin, you might want to spin various sizes of yarn—some big and fat, some smooth, some bumpy or thick and thin. Try plying some different sizes together if you are interested in creating unusual textures. If you ply a medium-sized handspun of one color with a fine strand of another color of handspun, you can create some interesting color and texture combinations. The two colors can be similar or contrasting depending on the effect you want.

By dyeing your fleece before you spin it, you then can spin several colors of fleece at the same time and get a single ply of multiple colors. Also, skeins of yarn that

101. *This detail photo illustrates a combination of techniques: a combination of horizontal stripes and hachures is woven in the stalk while irregular hatching highlights areas of the leaves. The tapestry was woven sideways.*

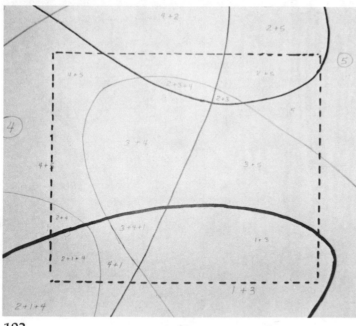

102.

103.

102. *This cartoon illustrates overlapping design areas that were used to create a transparent image.*

103. *A sample tapestry sometimes must be woven to ensure that the planned combinations will actually produce the expected transparent image. Here, five strands of weft were blended to achieve the transparent overlay image.*

have been inconsistently dyed (with some areas darker than others) offer beautiful subtle shading when woven.

You are not limited to wool and might want to try camel hair, alpaca, cotton, flax, or dog hair, to mention only a few possibilities. As you begin to weave tapestries with these various sizes, shapes, and textures of yarn, remember that each one will be handled differently during weaving and you may have to do some experimenting with the amount of bubbling necessary to maintain a flat surface and even edges. To find out more about spinning and dyeing your own materials, see the "Further Reading" chapter.

Now that you are familiar with the various tapestry

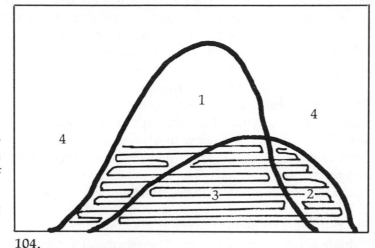

104. *Hatching can be used to create a transparent effect as long as the colors are of similar shades or the yarn is tweed, has texture, or is irregular in size.*

104.

105. *Yarns that are spun and dyed by hand give a tapestry special texture and color.*

105.

106.

106. *"Tidal Cascade" was woven with wool and mohair weft, which was hand spun and dyed with natural materials. Woven on a counterbalanced floor loom, the piece is twenty-six by thirty-six inches and has a wool warp set at six ends per inch. The piece was woven using traditional tapestry techniques, with the surface texture enhanced by Soumak and stitchery. Under the rock design, the back was padded with handmade felt to create an undulating effect. (Woven by Tigerlily Jones of Fort Bragg, California)*

techniques and the infinite possibilities for their use in your tapestries, let's take a look at the various ways of finishing and mounting your woven pieces. After that, you will be ready to browse through the "Inspiration" chapter to see what other weavers have done. Then it's on to the "Creating a Design" chapter.

6

FINISHING, MOUNTING, AND TAPESTRY CARE

SOME FINAL QUESTIONS

A beautifully woven tapestry can present a poor image if it is not nicely finished and mounted. Just as with the other apsects of tapestry weaving, you need to plan ahead and answer some final questions before putting the finishing touches on your creation. Where will the piece be hanging? Will it be a somewhat permanent location or will the tapestry be moved from place to place? Do you want the mounting rod to show?

The sample project presented some finishing techniques. This chapter explains some other methods. Remember, the technique you choose for one tapestry may not work well for another, so it is wise to be familiar with a variety of choices.

FINISHING

After steaming and blocking the tapestry (as instructed at the end of the "Now the Fun Begins" chapter), sew any slits that weaken the structure of the piece (see the "Slit" section in the "A Quick Review . . ." chapter). When you sew the slits together, work from the wrong side and use regular sewing thread. One-hundred-percent cotton thread is the strongest but is not always easy to find. Make a small stitch on one side of the slit, catching only a few rows of weft, then cross over to the other side of the slit and catch a few rows of weft along that edge. The stitches will disappear into the weft it you bring the thread straight across the slit as you make a stitch on the opposite side of the slit (fig. 108).

Trim any long weft ends on the back side of the tapestry to about one inch in length. When a weft has been woven around only one or two warp threads for quite a few rows, you might want to sew these weft ends back into the tapestry. Thread the weft end through a blunt-ended needle and sew it back into the tapestry in the direction of the warp.

Securing Warp Ends

Warp ends must be fastened in some way so that the weft does not "unweave." Tying double half-hitches around pairs of warp threads, as you did in the sample project (see the "Securing Warp Ends" section in the "Getting Ready to Weave" chapter), is quick and easy, and is worked while the piece is on the loom.

Four additional methods are presented here and each is worked after the tapestry has been removed from the loom. In the first method, you machine stitch along the edge of the tapestry. First, remove the piece from the loom, being sure to leave the warp ends about five or six inches long. This helps to keep the weft in place while you move the piece from the loom to the sewing machine, which I suggest you do immediately. Then sew several rows along the edge of the tapestry. I like to use both zigzag and straight stitching, sewing the rows right on top of one another.

In the second method, you tie pairs of warp ends together, either after you remove the tapestry from the loom or while you are removing it. Cut a few threads, being sure to leave them long enough so you can work with them, and tie them together, two at a time. Continue to cut and tie as you go.

In the third method, you cross individual warp threads over one another, forming a modified braid along the edge. To do this, place the tapestry right side down

107.

107. *Mounting a large tapestry sometimes can be a "breathtaking" experience. This piece was woven to match the angle of the ceiling, which vaults to twenty-six feet. The tapestry is about fifty-five square feet, with the largest panel being eleven feet long and forty-four inches wide. It was woven on a four-harness floor loom, and has a cotton warp set at six ends per inch and a wool weft. (Woven by the author)*

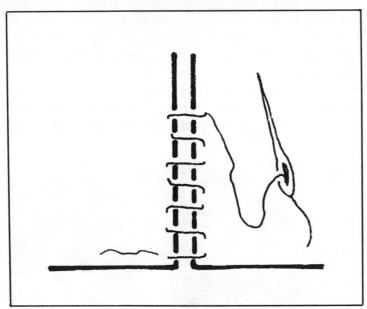

108.

108. *Vertical slits can be sewn together from the back of the tapestry.*

109. *Warp ends can be secured by forming a modified braid at the edge.*

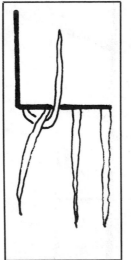

109A.

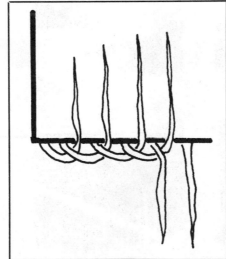

109B.

on a flat surface. Take warp thread two and cross it over warp one. Pull warp one up, toward the tapestry, and pull warp two down (fig. 109A). Pull snug and hold warp one in place while you continue. Take warp three over warp two and pull warp two up and warp three down. Continue across the width of the piece (fig. 109B). As you cross each warp over and pull it up, hold it in place until the next warp crossover takes place.

In the fourth method, you work each warp end back into the tapestry. If you choose to use this one, bubble the weft a little more on the first few rows of weaving so it is easier to work these ends back in. Also, be sure to leave the ends long enough so you can work with them. Working from the back of the piece, thread a large-eyed, blunt-ended needle with one warp end and work it into the tapestry in the space occupied by the warp next to it, as in figure 110. For example, thread warp one into the place occupied by warp two. Work warp end two in alongside warp three, and so on. Work each end back in about an inch, pull it until snug, and trim it close to the tapestry. The end will disappear into the weft.

By using this last technique, you can leave the piece unhemmed. This works very well, especially if you want the piece to be completely reversible. Remember, if you are going to leave the piece unhemmed, use a color of warp that is compatible with the weft, because a little will show along the edge.

The other three methods require hemming. After securing the warp ends, trim them so they are about one inch long. Tuck them under as you carefully sew the hem in place, using sewing thread or a strand of weft. When weaving, remember to allow at least one inch for the hem. This gives a flat finish to the edge and eliminates the rolled edge look that occurs if the hem is

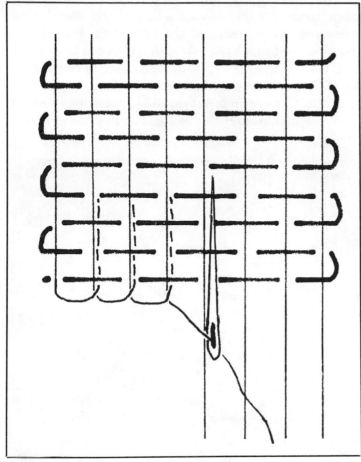

110.
too narrow.

MOUNTING

There are also a number of ways to mount your tapestry. At the top edge of the piece, you can weave a hem that is large enough to form a woven casing when it is folded down. You then can slip a rod or flat board

111.

through the casing (fig. 111).

Velcro gives a nice finish and works well when you want the piece to hang flat against the wall. After hemming the tapestry, attach one strip of Velcro to the back of the piece by stitching along the top and bottom edge of the Velcro with sewing thread. Sew the soft or loop side of the Velcro to the tapestry, then attach the other side of the strip, which is the "hook" side and the stiffer of the two strips, to the wall with tacks or staples. Then place the tapestry against this strip and the two pieces of Velcro grip each other, holding the tapestry securely in place (fig. 112).

Adhesive Velcro is also available but somewhat harder to find. This consists of the "hook" side of regular Velcro, but instead of having a second strip, it has an adhesive backing that sticks to most surfaces.

110. *In another method of securing warp ends, the ends are woven back into the tapestry. Each one is worked into the place that is occupied by its neighbor.*

111. *A large woven hem can form a casing for the mounting rod.*

The fibers of the woven piece grasp the Velcro. This is ideal for hanging pieces that are bound on all four edges, such as Navajo rugs, and pieces that are irregular in shape (fig. 113).

Tip: If you cannot find adhesive Velcro, just tack the "hook" side of regular Velcro to the wall and press the tapestry to it. These little "hooks" will grab the wool and hang on.

Another way of mounting a tapestry is to make a fabric casing for the mounting board, and insert screw eyes along the top edge of the board (fig. 114). To do this, you need to select a fabric that does not have much give, such as weaver's K cloth, velveteen, or fine corduroy. The process I then use is as follows:

1. Cut a strip of fabric wide enough to go under and around the board. For this example, the

112. *Attaching Velcro to the tapestry and the wall makes a secure mounting.*

113. *Using adhesive Velcro solves the problem of hanging an irregular-shaped piece. The adhesive back of the single Velcro strip attaches to the wall and the front side of the strip, which has a "hooked" texture, grasps the fibers of the tapestry.*

112.

113.

board is 1¼ inches by ⅜ inch, so a piece of fabric 4 inches wide will do. Cut the strip 1½ inches longer than the length of the mounting board, which is slightly shorter than the width of the tapestry.

2. Working from the wrong side of the tapestry, place the fabric so it extends 2½ inches past the top of the tapestry.
3. Using sewing thread, stitch the fabric ⅝ inch down from the top of the tapestry (fig. 115) and along the lower edge, being sure the stitches do not go through to the right side of the tapestry.
4. Place the lower edge of the mounting board a little above point A in figure 115. Loosely fold the fabric over the top of the board, fold in the ends, and staple it in place. Turn the board down one turn and stitch the layers of fabric together at the ends and all along the bottom of the mounting board.
5. Place two screw eyes in the top edge of the board, through the cloth, and the tapestry is ready to hang.

It is not necessary for the casing to go around the board completely, but I like this method, because it puts a piece of fabric between the wood and the tapestry. On a small tapestry, you might make a shell casing out of a piece of ribbon or bias twill tape. Do not sew the casing perfectly flat—leave enough room so that the mounting board can be inserted easily. If the casing is too snug, the tapestry will roll when the mounting board is inserted, and the tapestry will not lie flat.

Using fabric and Velcro is probably one of the most efficient, if not the quickest and easiest way, to mount a tapestry. It is especially good for large pieces and pieces

114.

that are woven sideways. The process is as follows:
1. Sew the soft piece (the loop side) of the Velcro to the back of the tapestry, along both edges of the Velcro. Place the Velcro about ¾ inch down from the top of the tapestry.
2. Completely wrap the mounting board with a piece of fabric and staple it in place.
3. Place the stiff side of the Velcro along the full length of the mounting board (on the side

114. *In another method of mounting a tapestry, a fabric casing is sewn to the tapestry and then folded around the mounting board. Screw eyes are inserted at the top of the board for mounting.*

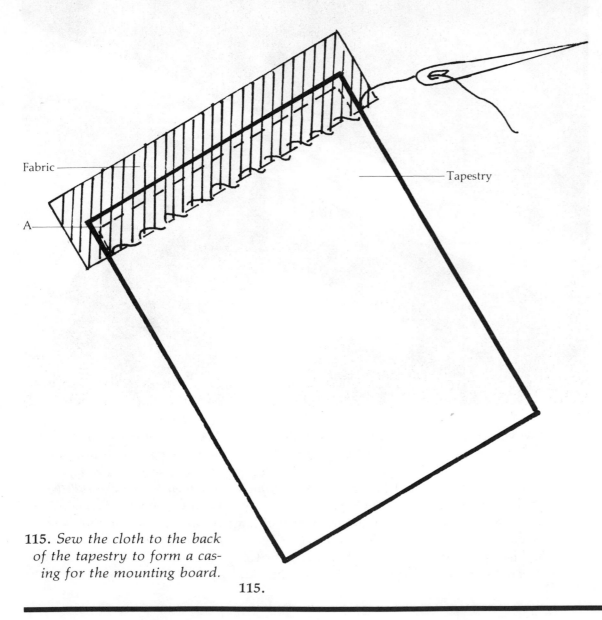

Fabric

A

Tapestry

115. *Sew the cloth to the back of the tapestry to form a casing for the mounting board.*

115.

where you stapled the fabric in place) and staple the Velcro about every two inches.

4. Put two screw eyes along the top edge of the mounting board, and you're all finished.

This process keeps the mounting board separate from the tapestry and makes it easy to hang, ship, and store because the tapestry can be rolled up and stored separately from the mounting board. To hang the piece, simply put a couple of nails in the wall, hang the mounting board, and then press the tapestry to the mounting board—the two Velcro strips will form a secure bond.

Tapestries woven in shapes other than squares or rectangles create special challenges. One example is shown in figure 116. This tapestry was designed to hang free and be viewed from all sides. It was woven sideways and the hem was woven wide enough to form a self-casing along both sides and the top edge. A flexible rod was inserted in the casing, forming the curved shape. To keep the piece flat, two metal rods were wrapped with weft yarn and attached to the back of the piece, becoming part of the design.

On large pieces I like to make a casing at the bottom, also. By slipping a metal strip through the casing, a little extra weight is added to the piece. This is especially helpful in cases in which the tapestry is woven sideways.

TAPESTRY CARE

Taking proper care of a tapestry is really quite painless. First of all, do not hang it directly in the sunlight, as this will cause a gradual fading and may eventually cause the materials to deteriorate. Keeping a tapestry clean also is no problem. In most cases, a gentle vacuuming once in a while is all the piece needs. I have never used a silicone-spray treatment to help keep a tapestry clean, but I know some people who use this process on every piece they weave.

If for some reason the tapestry gets dirty (which it probably will not), one of the best ways to clean it is to wash it with cold water. Generally a soap is not needed, but if it is, be sure it is gentle. Before washing, measure the size of the tapestry—it will be necessary to block it back to this size after washing. If you place the tapestry on a screen that is elevated a little, then spray it with cold water (a garden hose works fine), the soiled water will wash right through the piece. Block it to size, smoothing it with your hands, and leave it in place until it is completely dry.

If you are considering dry cleaning, keep in mind that the piece might shrink during this process. The amount of shrinkage will vary, depending on the materials used, the size and set of the warp, the size and kind of weft, and how tight the piece is woven. The amount of skrinkage in the direction of the warp is less than the shrinkage in the direction of the weft. The tighter the piece is woven, the less it will shrink. You might want to do some experimenting with some small samples to see if, and how much, they shrink.

When working with wool, there is always concern about moths. Most good quality weaving yarns are mothproofed by one of two commercial processes: one in which the yarn is sprayed and the other in which it is dipped in a mothproofing solution. The dipped process seems to provide better protection against moths. When you buy the yarn, ask how it was mothproofed.

If you are using handspun, you will have to treat it yourself. I have never encountered any problems with moths, but by being aware of a potential problem, you may be able to eliminate it before it gets out of hand. Mothproofing sprays that are very effective can be purchased at most weaving supply stores, and sprayed on

116.

116. *"Rainbow Lorikeet" was designed to be viewed from all sides so all weft ends were woven in. It was woven sideways on a floor loom, then the mounting supports were wrapped with weft and attached to one side of the tapestry. The piece is thirty-three by twenty inches and has a cotton 3/2 warp set at six ends per inch and a wool weft.*

your tapestry.

When storing tapestries or transporting them from one area to another, roll them rather than folding them. You will be surprised how quickly a crease can form and how difficult it is to remove it.

A.

B.

C.

A. *"In Memoriam/Innerscape"*
by Noël Bennett

B. *"Waves Returning" by*
Henry W. Hallett

C. *"Night Bloom" by Nancy*
Harvey

Plate 1

A.

B.

A. *"Dawn's Beginning" by Audrey Moore*

B. *"Burning Tower" by Katherine Kilgore*

Plate 2

B.

A.

A. *"White Petunias" by Mark Adams; woven by the San Francisco Tapestry Workshop*

B. *"Riftvalley Volcano" by Silvia Heyden*

Plate 3

A.

A. *"Not Unlike Here" by Alix Peshette*

B. *"Silver Canyon" by Michelle Lester*

C. *"Light Flower" by Yael Lurie; woven by Jean-Pierre Larochette*

B.

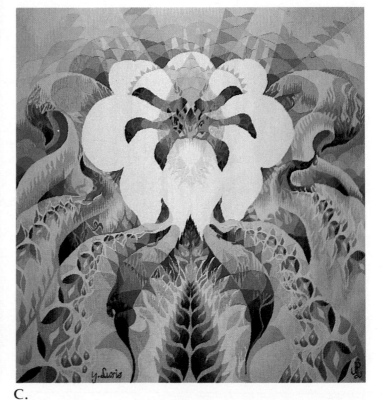

C.

Plate 4

7 INSPIRATION

As we begin to explore tapestry and as we continue to grow, a great deal can be learned by looking around and seeing what is being done by others. The purpose of this chapter is to expose you to a variety of tapestry styles, techniques, and materials, all of which are used to create beautiful tapestries that reflect individuality and creativity.

When I began weaving tapestries, I was always inspired (and still am) by the beautiful pieces woven by others, but I also found it somewhat frustrating initially—the photographs did not tell how a piece was woven, what materials were used, and what techniques had created all those interesting and unusual special effects. Therefore, this chapter includes—along with photographs, the title of each tapestry, and the weavers' names—additional information regarding materials and looms used as well as remarks by some of the weavers. Color photographs are referred to by plate numbers and are included in the color section of this book. Black-and-white photographs are referred to by figure numbers and are included in this chapter. Tapestries are designed by the weaver unless otherwise noted.

"White Petunias" (plate 3A), by Mark Adams of San Francisco, was woven in the traditional Aubusson technique. It was woven by the San Francisco Tapestry Workshop in 1978 on an Aubusson low warp tapestry loom. The tapestry is fifty-two by forty-one inches and the cotton warp was set at thirteen portee. Portee is the French measurement of warp set based on centimeter measurement of warp sections. When thirteen portee is converted, it equals approximately 9.9 warp ends per inch. The weft is all wool and several strands of weft were used together as a single weft during weaving. A full-scale cartoon was used and the piece was woven from the back.

Noël Bennett of Corrales, New Mexico, wove "In Memoriam/Innerscape" (plate 1A) on a Navajo loom using Navajo techniques. The tapestry is six and one-half by three and one-half feet with a wool warp set at eight ends per inch. "It was begun with the intent to merge Navajo and Persian elements—thereby integrating a just culminated eight-year experience on the Navajo reservation with a Lebanese heritage. All weft colors were hand dyed, and chenille was selected as the weft for its pile and for its rayon/cotton, shiny/dull qualities. It was woven on an upright Navajo loom to allow the artist full view of the composition, thereby encouraging the best color and design decisions possible."

Pamela Patrie of Portland, Oregon, weaves on a large upright frame loom that has a large heddle bar for shed changes and is similar to the Gobelin tapestry looms. "Fuji Fuji" (fig. 117) is four by six feet and was woven on a heavy cotton warp set at four ends per inch, with a wool weft forming the thick texture. "Spontaneity is a main theme in my work. Weaving on an upright frame loom, the tapestry is woven from the back side. I use large mirrors to view the piece as I weave. I often walk to the front side to study the composition. If I can't arrive at a solution this way, I then do color drawings and paintings on paper."

Combining various techniques is the way Judith McNally-Warner of Fabius, New York, creates a feeling

117. "Fuji Fuji" by Pamela Patrie. (Photo by Elmer Zook)

118. "Landscape Tapestry" by Judith McNally-Warner

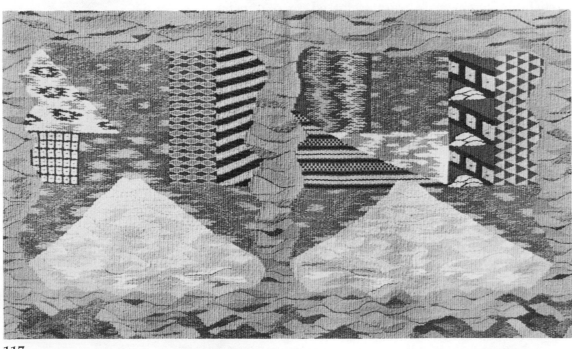

117.

118.

of distance in her tapestries, as illustrated in "Landscape Tapestry" (fig. 118). It was woven on a floor loom using a 10/2 linen warp set at six ends per inch double, and hand-dyed wool was used for the weft. Since color plays an important role in her pieces, Judith prefers to dye her yarns to get exactly the color she wants. The tapestry is thirty-two by twenty-seven inches. "Color, texture, and layering are all used to create a feeling of foreground and background. The waterfall and tree trunks are knotted."

119.

119. *"Pastoral" by Hal Painter*

Hal Painter lives in Oregon and it perhaps was the quiet countryside in Chiloquin that offered inspiration for his tapestry "Pastoral" (fig. 119). It was woven on a counterbalanced floor loom with an overhead beater. The warp in this piece is 8/4 cotton set at nine ends per inch and the weft is wool. The tapestry is forty-eight and one-half by thirty and one-half inches.

"Not Unlike Here" (plate 4A) is a tapestry by Alix Peshette of Fair Oaks, California. She uses a small-scale cartoon during weaving, measuring and marking key points on the warp as she weaves. This thirty-two-inch by seventy-inch tapestry was woven on a four-harness jack-type floor loom using a cotton warp set at six ends per inch. The weft is a combination of handspun and commercial wools.

"Light Flower" (plate 4C) is another tapestry woven in the traditional Aubusson technique. Jean-Pierre Larochette of Berkeley, California, wove this piece,

120. *"African Cascades" by Silvia Heyden*

121. *"Drifting" by Maggie Potter*

122. *"Domain of the Indian Leaf Bird" by Katherine Kilgore*

120.

which was designed by his wife, Yael Lurie. It was woven on an Aubusson low warp tapestry loom with a cotton warp set at thirteen portee. The weft is wool and silk and the piece is fifty-two and three-quarters by forty-seven inches.

Silvia Heyden of Durham, North Carolina, wove "African Cascades" (fig. 120) on an upright (vertical) tapestry loom. This piece is seven by eleven feet, the warp is 10/5 linen set at six ends per inch, and the weft is linen and wool.

Moving from a very large piece to a very small piece, we can see that size is not important, as illustrated by "Drifting" (fig. 121), a tapestry by Maggie Potter of Martinez, California. Measuring six by eight inches, this tapestry was woven on a floor loom using a linen warp set at fifteen ends per inch and a hand-dyed wool weft.

"Burning Tower" (plate 2B), by Katherine Kilgore of San Francisco, uses a cotton warp set at ten ends per inch and Persian needlepoint yarn for the weft. The tapestry is forty-four by forty-eight inches. "I work on a

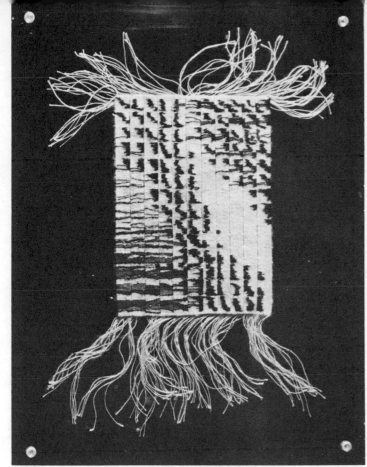

121.

high warp loom of my own construction. When I work, I try to capture my inner vision in small color sketches, to keep these images sharp, fresh, and alive. I do not use a cartoon to work from, but allow myself plenty of room to improvise, at the same time referring back to my small sketch. It is important to me that the piece radiate its own inner life." Another tapestry by Katherine Kilgore is "Domain of the Indian Leaf Bird" (fig. 122). It is forty-four by forty-eight inches and also uses a cotton warp, this time set at eight ends per inch.

122.

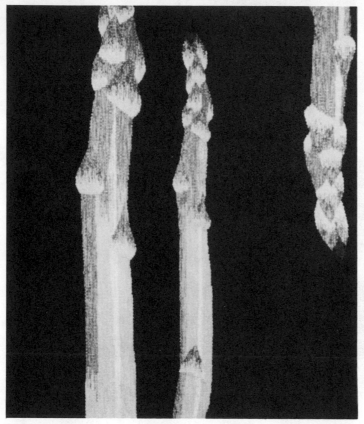

123. *"Asparagus" by Judi Keen*

124. *"Facets" by Jim Brown*

123.

Once again the weft is Persian needlepoint yarn.

"Asparagus" (fig. 123), a thirty-six-inch by forty-five-inch tapestry by Judi Keen of Sacramento, California, was woven on a jack-type floor loom using cotton seine twine (8/2/3) set at six ends per inch and a wool weft. It was woven in the Aubusson tapestry technique.

Jim Brown of Chiloquin, Oregon, also used a modified Aubusson tapestry technique in weaving "Facets" (fig. 124), which is thirty-one by twenty-eight

124.

inches. Jim used an 8/4/4 cotton warp set at nine ends per inch and Paternayan wool for the weft. The tapestry was woven on a counterbalanced floor loom.

"Riftvalley Volcano" (plate 3B) is by Silvia Heyden of Durham, North Carolina. "The tapestry loom is an instrument which the tapestry weaver has to learn to understand before she can use its specific vocabulary for her own design ideas in order to come as close as possible to the unique expression of tapestry." This piece is fifty by sixty-eight inches and was woven on an upright tapestry loom using a 10/5 linen warp and a cotton and linen weft.

Beatrice Meachum of Lagunitas, California, also worked on an upright tapestry loom, using traditional French tapestry techniques, in weaving "Guardian of the East" (fig. 125). The cotton warp was set at thirteen portee. The weft is CUM tapestry wool and silk and was all naturally dyed. The dyeing techniques included spaced dyed skeins and Kasuri Ikat. Note the warp threads still at the edges. The piece has just been removed from the loom and has not been hemmed. The tapestry was woven in a sideways direction from the back. Beatrice placed a full-scale cartoon of the design behind the warp during weaving.

The double weft interlock technique was used by Henry W. Hallett of Pittsburgh, Pennsylvania, when he wove "Waves Returning" (plate 1B). This piece is thirty by forty-four inches, the warp is cotton set at five ends per inch, and the weft is wool and rayon. "I weave on a forty-five-inch four-harness jack-type loom. I work in the double weft interlock technique, which necessitates weaving the entire width of the warp before moving on to the next row. It enables the use of the beater the loom is equipped with to pack the weft in place. It also makes it possible to weave vertical divisions of color areas going the entire length of the piece without ending up with a lot of separate strips, which need to be sewn together later. And most of all, it gives me a sense of graceful and continuous growth and movement."

Choosing another tapestry technique, Ellie Fidler of Berkeley, California, weaves her pieces entirely in Soumak, as shown in "Midwinter Interval" (fig. 126). Measuring six feet by four and one-half feet, it was woven on a six-foot Swedish floor loom. This tapestry

125.

125. *"Guardian of the East" by Beatrice Meachum. (Photo by Friday Forsthoff)*

has a wool-mohair warp set at six and one-half ends per inch and the weft is wool. "In each tapestry I experiment with one element, which always keeps something new going on and I can see how it behaves in the context of the direction of color, image, and technique in which I am moving. An important variable always presents enough of a risk to make a tapestry—a work of months—exciting. In recent tapestries I began using a color join in the Soumak simply for the effect of the cleft. There is no color change yet a join is used for its value as a line."

Combining a variety of weft materials, Michelle Lester of New York City used wool, metallic yarns, and silk in her eight-inch-square tapestry "Silver Canyon" (plate 4B). The piece was woven on a four-harness floor loom using a 12/2 linen for the warp, which was set at twelve ends per inch.

Again, choosing to work on a Navajo loom, Audrey Moore of Clackamas, Oregon, wove "Dawn's Beginning" (plate 2A) with hand-spun and hand-dyed wool weft. The dyes included indigo, madder, and cochineal. The warp, also wool, was set at eight ends per inch. The piece is fifty-six by seventy inches.

The Southwest was the inspiration for my tapestry "Night Bloom" (plate 1C). The oversized blooms are superimposed on a typical Southwest landscape, creating a dual view. The bloom of the sacred datura plant folds and wilts in the heat of the desert sun but remains in full bloom all night. A combination of traditional and contemporary techniques was used. The tapestry is four by five feet and was woven on a sixty-inch four-harness floor loom using a cotton warp set at six ends per inch and a wool weft.

Combine the techniques, materials, and loom you like to create the feel you want your tapestries to have. As you can see from the options presented in this chapter, the possibilities are unlimited. Now it's your turn to create your own design. The next chapter, "Creating a Design," will give you lots of ideas and help you get started.

126. *"Midwinter Interval" by Ellie Fidler*

126.

8

CREATING A DESIGN

HELPFUL COMMENTS FOR EVERYONE
Designing your own tapestries is possible whether or not you have a background in art. For those of you who do have an art background, designing a tapestry is just an extension of your talent into another form of expression. Here are a few comments that might be helpful as you start designing your first few tapestries.

The size of the tapestry is not important. A good tapestry is determined by its design and craftsmanship. Keep the image simple to begin with, using colors rather than lines to break up an area. Consider where the tapestry will hang. Subtle shading that is pleasing when seen up close will disappear if the piece is viewed from a distance. Remember, horizontal lines are easier to weave than vertical warp-way lines. Gradual curves thus can be woven very smoothly when they are horizontal. This is difficult to achieve with vertical lines unless the warp is spaced very close together.

Prepare your cartoon with as much or as little detail as you feel you need. Some weavers prefer to prepare the cartoon in exact detail, having everything worked out before weaving begins, while others prefer a minimum amount of drawing and do most of their designing during weaving.

If you choose to use a colored cartoon, remember that such materials as paints and crayons cannot reproduce the exact color and soft appearance of yarn. You will have to try to visualize what it is going to look like. If this is difficult in the beginning, weave some color samples. (The process used in the traditional French Aubusson technique involves not only the weaving of color samples, but also the weaving of a sample section of the tapestry before the actual weaving of the tapestry begins.) Perhaps the most important consideration is that this is a woven piece—do not try to make it look like something else.

For those of you who come from a nonart background and are saying, "I can't draw," the first thing to do is reword that phrase. Try something like "I have never drawn anything" or "I have never taken an art class." One of these is probably a truer statement. The following thoughts about designing a tapestry will help you get started. There are many books about color and design that can help you, also. You might even want to take some art or design classes after you become familiar with a few basics.

As you begin to think about design, concentrate on something that is of interest to you. Start simple—maybe a landscape (fig. 127) or a simple stripe or Navajo design (fig. 128) or an abstract of curves and angles (fig. 129)—building as your experience and confidence grow. Most people cannot simply close their eyes and get a full-blown idea for a tapestry (or any other) design. Only a genius can do that. What about the rest of us? Ideas grow from the inspirations around us. Now that you

128.

127. *Landscape scenes are another good subject for beginners, offering many soft gradual lines. "Distant Pyramid" was woven with a handspun wool weft. Sagebrush was the only dye material used to get the various shades of green and yellow that make up the entire composition of the tapestry. Tin, chrome, and copper were used as mordants.*

128. *Begin with a simple design, perhaps even some stripes as illustrated in this Navajo "Chief Blanket" pattern. (Woven on a Navajo loom by the author)*

127.

have an interest in weaving tapestries and are concerned about design, you will be surprised how many things you see in a different way. As you look around, stop and take a closer look. Notice colors, relationships, proportions, lines, shapes, and so on. Look at books, magazines, advertisements, posters, brochures, sunsets, mountains, landscapes, animals, objects—the sources of inspiration are endless.

Do some research to remind yourself how things really look. Cut out pictures or parts of pictures or designs that you like (even some you do not like). Try to figure out what attracts you to each one, looking at the lines, shapes, colors, and textures of each. Start a research notebook, grouping these design inspirations by subject matter.

DESIGNING TECHNIQUES

Putting the first mark on paper is usually the most difficult step in creating a design. When I took my first tapestry weaving class, we had a great time creating designs from objects and cut paper, which made the designing process much easier. This section includes some of the same techniques.

The first couple of them involve preparing a full-scale cartoon. Start by cutting a piece of paper the size you want the tapestry to be. In these first two examples—one using an object, the other using cut paper—let's use a sample size of twelve by eighteen inches.

Select an object with an interesting shape. The kitchen and the barn are full of such things. Or take a walk outside—through the woods or around the block—and see what you can find. Once you have chosen the object, place it on the paper and draw around it. Continue placing it in different places and directions, overlapping it here and there. You might want to make several different cartoons, combining different objects. After all the outlines are on the paper, color the various shapes and parts of shapes, and you have a design ready to weave.

You can use cut paper several ways to create a design. One way is to use colored paper. Cut out different shapes and make a collage, rearranging the shapes until you get the effect you like. Then paste them in place and you have a completed design.

Cutting a shape from folded paper is the process I used for my first tapestry design. Fold a piece of paper that is one-third the size of the total design size (four by eighteen inches in this case), then cut a design (just like paper dolls and snowflakes). Unfold this cut-out shape, place it on the drawing paper, and draw around it as you did with the object. I used the cut-out image at both edges of the paper and then changed the direction and overlapped it in other areas. After coloring the areas, use a dark felt pen to outline them so they are easy to see when the cartoon is placed under the warp. The sample

129.

129. *Abstracts can offer further development in your design growth, using large and small design areas, curves, and angles in the same piece. This tapestry is four by two and one-half feet.*

paper shape, my cartoon, and the tapestry are shown in figure 130.

To create a design from one of the "inspirations" you have collected and placed in your research notebook, you will need some tracing paper and a felt pen. Select one of the designs you like and trace only the areas that are of interest to you. Which design shapes appeal to you most? Change the tracing so you like it better. Working with a series of tracing-paper overlays, continue to change the design, bringing forward the part of the design you like, until you have a final design. Using this technique allows you to change the design until you like it, without having to recreate the entire image with each revision (fig. 131).

130. *Cutting shapes out of paper* (center) *and drawing around them as they are placed in different positions on the cartoon* (right) *is one way of creating a design for a tapestry* (left).

131. *Experiment with tracing-paper overlays* (left). *As the design develops (steps one through four), only the areas the designer wants as part of the final design are traced onto the next revision. Other areas are redesigned, with some experimenting with color sometimes done along the way. The final design* (right) *is photocopied several times, allowing for experimentation with various color combinations. The end result, the finished tapestry, is shown in color plate 4A.*

130.

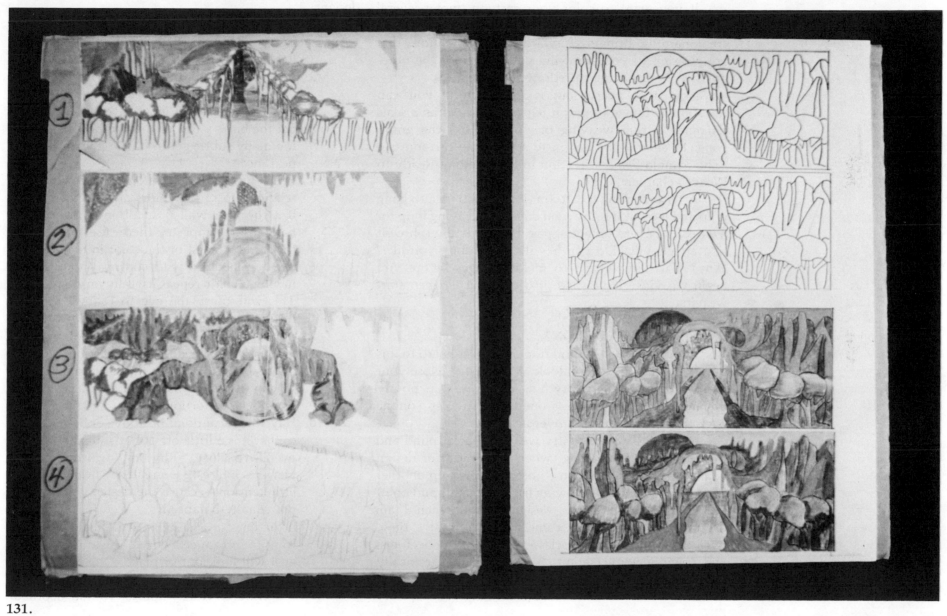

131.

If you want to color your cartoon, make several photocopies. This will allow you to try various color combinations, bringing forward the combinations that are pleasing to you, allowing you to recolor the other areas without having to redraw the design.

Now that everything is just perfect, you can transfer the image to graph paper and use it as a scale reference during weaving or you can use the graph paper to enlarge the design to a full-scale cartoon (see "The Sample Project" section in the "Getting Ready to Weave" chapter).

After preparing a cartoon, it is a good idea to hang it up and look at it for several days. Try leaving it up for a week and every time you pass by, think about how it first affects you. Do you like it? What don't you like? Why? This allows you to make changes before you begin weaving. If you like it the way it is, then start weaving.

WHAT IS GOOD DESIGN?

I think the most helpful response I ever heard to this question was "If you can look at a tapestry, close your eyes, and remember everything about it, it is poorly designed. A good design is one that you keep coming back to look at over and over again."

Regardless of a tapestry weaver's background and training prior to weaving, when the subject of design comes up, he or she listens, hoping to pick up another idea or tip. I find the following list of thoughts and opinions regarding color and design helpful when I am designing. The comments came mostly one at a time, over the years, through classes, workshops, lectures, and friendly conversation. Most of them specifically deal with design and color as they relate to tapestry weaving. Think about them as you create your tapestry designs:

1. Color is not important—the value relationship is. (The value tells us whether the color is light or dark.)
2. Use a dark background to add richness, allow depth, and create an appearance of activity. It also can make up for what the design lacks.
3. Set the basic value of the composition. Using too many subtle colors can create a faded appearance.
4. Every time you add a color, you weaken the relationship of the colors already there.
5. If a room or wall is small and you want to hang a large tapestry there, use the color of the wall for most of the color in the tapestry.
6. Create repetition with contrast in a piece by having a color repeat itself in varying shades. This will cause the eye to follow the color throughout the piece.
7. Simplify the design and use few colors. Limitations allow freedom of expression.
8. If possible, design with the cartoon on a wall, so you can stand back and look at it.
9. Consider proportion.
10. Have the focal point be above or below center so that it is a little offset but still maintains an overall balance. Rhythm, which holds a viewer's interest, is created when there is a little tension because the design elements are not equally balanced.
11. If the lines in a design are all angles and you want to introduce a curve, use more than one or it will look out of place.
12. Avoid using identical symmetrical shapes.
13. Use textures to say things, to add depth or

132.

132. *Landscapes can offer more advanced design challenges as illustrated in "Summer Oaks," which was mounted on a concave support to add depth to its appearance. Handspun wools, dog hair, silk, and Karakul wool were used for weft. The wool warp was set at five ends per inch. The tapestry is nineteen by forty-one inches. (Woven by Sylvia Tessore of Sacramento, California)*

create dimension.

14. Make your tapestry look as though it could not have been represented as well in any other medium.
15. Love it and let it show.

Everyone you meet will have different thoughts and other points of view. Write them down. If a comment is thought-provoking (whether you agree or disagree), it is worthwhile and will help you grow, building ideas for better and better design.

So many things around us offer inspiration. I know if I could weave tapestries for the next twenty years (and I plan to), I would not have time to try all the ideas that are floating around in my imagination and noted on little pieces of paper here and there. I know this is why I have become so intrigued with weaving. No matter how much I learn, there are still so many fascinating challenges.

I hope I have stirred your imagination and inspired you to explore the endless possibilities of tapestry weaving. As you do so, let your imagination run wild. Experiment, create, and—most of all—enjoy!

9

SOURCES OF WEAVING SUPPLIES

Today, many cities throughout the United States have weaving shops that carry all the necessary tools, equipment, and supplies that weavers require. Many needlepoint and knitting shops also carry basic weaving supplies—portable looms, shuttles, combs, and Persian and Paternayan yarns, which are ideal for tapestry weaving. If your area does not have any such shops and you are unable to locate any through the telephone directory, the Handweavers Guild of America publishes a suppliers' directory. It lists firms that specialize in supplies and equipment for weaving, spinning, and dyeing, and also indicates which ones handle mail orders. You can order a copy of this directory through HGA Publications, P.O. Box 7-374, West Hartford, Connecticut 06107.

The following list also will be helpful in obtaining information about looms. For your convenience, I first have listed manufacturers who make small portable tapestry looms as well as larger looms, and have marked the names with an asterisk. To the best of my knowledge, the remaining manufacturers on the list make only floor looms and larger looms. However, if you write to them, you can get an up-to-date list of what each has to offer.

*Beka Looms
1648 Grand Avenue
St. Paul, Minnesota 55105

*Brittany Looms
3461 Big Cut Road
Placerville, California 95667

*Crisp Woodworking
333 Southeast Third Street
Portland, Oregon 97214

*Fiber Designer Loom
1836 Candelaria Northwest
Albuquerque, New Mexico 87107

*Glimåkra Looms
P.O. Box 16157
19285 Detroit Road
Rocky River, Ohio 44116

*Golden Looms
School Products Company
1201 Broadway
New York, New York 10001

*Leclerc Corporation
Highway 9, North
P.O. Box 491
Plattsburgh, New York 12901

*Leclerc West
P.O. Box 408
19658 Eighth Street East
Sonoma, California 95476

*Macomber Looms
Beech Ridge Road
York, Maine 03909

*Ram Loom
400 First Avenue
Minneapolis, Minnesota 55401

*Schacht Spindle Company
P.O. Box 2157 K
Boulder, Colorado 80306

Arachne Looms
Box 174
White Fish, Montana 59937

Cascade Looms
7364 Conifer Northeast
Salem, Oregon 97303

Cranbrook Weaving Loom
Heritage Woodcrafts, Inc.
2470 Dixie Highway
Pontiac, Michigan 48055

Gilmore Looms
1032 North Broadway
Stockton, California 95205

Harrisville Designs
Harrisville, New Hampshire 03450

Herald Looms
130 Lee Street
Lodi, Ohio 44254

J-Made Looms
P.O. Box 452
Oregon City, Oregon 97045

Northwest Looms
P.O. Box 10369
Bainbridge Island, Washington 98110

Norwood Looms
P.O. Box 167 S
Freemont, Michigan 49419

Studio Handcrafts
5405 Aura Avenue
P.O. Box 686
Tarzana, California 91356

Thought Products
R.D. No. 2
Somerset, Pennsylvania 15501

10

FURTHER READING

BOOKS

Bennett, Noël. *Designing with the Wool: Advanced Techniques in Navajo Weaving.* Flagstaff, Arizona: Northland Press, 1979. Begins where *Working with the Wool* left off. It includes many advanced Navajo techniques along with many graphed Navajo design patterns to assist the weaver in the preparation and execution of a beautifully woven Navajo piece.

Bennett, Noël, and Bighorse, Tiana. *Working with the Wool.* Flagstaff, Arizona: Northland Press, 1971. Gives detailed instructions about Navajo weaving. It includes descriptions of tools and techniques, step-by-step instructions for weaving a sample project, and instructions for building your own loom.

Broudy, Eric. *The Book of Looms: A History of the Handloom from Ancient Times to the Present.* New York: Van Nostrand Reinhold, 1979. Presents the history of the handloom. Photographs of the looms used by many cultures throughout history are included.

Brown, Rachel. *The Weaving, Spinning, and Dyeing Book.* New York: Alfred A. Knopf, 1979. Gives instructions for more than fifty projects, detailed information about a wide variety of weaving techniques, and tips on spinning, dyeing, design, weaving methods, equipment, and tools. It also has over four hundred illustrations.

Ingers, Gertrud. *Flemish Weaving: A Guide to Tapestry Technique.* New York: Van Nostrand Reinhold Company, 1971. Emphasizes the Flemish techniques and equipment used in tapestry weaving. Many color photographs are included, and cartoons for weaving small tapestries are in a pocket in the back of the book.

Simmons, Paula. *Spinning and Weaving with Wool.* Seattle: Pacific Search Press, 1977. Presents all the essentials for making you a successful spinner and weaver of handspun wool. In addition to step-by-step instructions on all phases of the spinning process, detailed instructions are provided to help you build your own equipment.

Thompson, Francis Paul. *Tapestry: Mirror of History.* New York: Crown Publishers, 1980. Describes the art of tapestry making from all periods and regions, including the Far East, South America, and Europe. Many tapestries are illustrated in its fifty color plates and seventy-seven black-and-white photographs.

Verlet, Pierre. *The Book of Tapestry*. New York: The Vendome Press, 1978. Follows the history of tapestry as an art form from the Middle Ages to the present, and includes eighty-two color plates of tapestries covering this span of tapestry history.

MAGAZINES
Fiberarts Magazine (50 College Street, Asheville, North Carolina 28801) is published bimonthly. Its articles cover the fiber and fiber-related fields in general and are informational rather than instructional.

Handwoven (Interweave Press, 306 North Washington, Loveland, Colorado 80537) is published five times a year and emphasizes woven works. It is informational and also provides detailed technical instructions for many handwoven projects.

Shuttle Spindle and Dyepot (Handweavers Guild of America, P.O. Box 7-374, West Hartford, Connecticut 06107) is published quarterly and covers a wide range of information relating to fiber, weaving, spinning, and dyeing.

The Weaver's Journal (The Colorado Fiber Center, P.O. Box 2049, Boulder, Colorado 80306) is published four times a year. It emphasizes "how-to" information, including many projects that usually are for loom-controlled weaves.

Most of these magazines also include information about shows and exhibits, interviews with people working in fiber and fiber-related fields, book reviews, and historical information.

INDEX